21ST CENTURY PEOPLE LEADERSHIP

21 POWER TOOLS FOR GETTING BIG RESULTS OUT OF YOUR TEAM, STARTING RIGHT NOW

Dave Stitt & Paul Fox

Published by 21CPL Productions
© 2010 Dave Stitt and Paul Fox

ISBN- 978-0-9567747-0-5

Edited by Rod Sweet
Book design by Doriane Laithier
Cartoons by Huw Aaron

Printed and bound in Great Britain by Short Run Press Ltd.
Bittern Road, Sowton Industrial Estate, Exeter EX2 7LW

Yet more praise for
21ST CENTURY PEOPLE LEADERSHIP

*"This book is an essential read for both the new and experienced leader
alike. It provides the reader with a series of unique tools from which to steer
the ship whilst at the same time reaching a high level of performance at
both individual and team level. After reading this book your glass will never
ever be 'half empty' again."*
Rob Adams, MD, Birse Civils Ltd.

*"The fact that Paul and Dave are both successful in business, fit as fiddles,
have good family lives and find the time to write this book is a strong
indicator that they have it sorted. Not only do they follow their own advice
on leading, they've managed to communicate it in their own direct energetic
and effective style."*
Malcolm Ellis, MD, Aedas Architects Ltd.

*"I've worked with Dave for over 15 years. His enthusiasm and belief in his
subject come through in 21 short, easy-to-digest chapters that simplify the
art of leadership - a great read for new and experienced leaders alike."*
Mark Thompson, MD, Ryder Architecture

*"DSA have done some great coaching with my business and the tools we
acquired during those sessions are still used every day. As a leader I'm
always looking for inspiration and ways to inspire my team. This book offers
some brilliant tools to do exactly that, with straightforward methods to deal
with the business issues that hold us back. It also gives you tools to help
build that 'tight' team to ensure project success on any scale."*
Tony Whelan, MD, Whelan Construction

"Excellent! '21st Century People Leadership' captures the essence of good leadership and delivers what many of us seek: the way to improved performance. Acknowledging that the answer stares back at you in the mirror is the first step. This is one of those books you'll want to write your name in to prevent it from going astray. Dave and Paul have delivered an excellent reference you'll consult for the rest of your working life."
Stuart Mansley, Divisional Operations Director, Dean & Dyball Civil Engineering

"Dave and Paul are helping our senior team development and I believe this book catches the flavour, simplicity and directness of their approach, supported by practical advice and sound theory. I will be putting a copy in each team member's Christmas box."
Seamus A. Keogh, CEO, ClancyDocwra Ltd.

"International Business School in one easy volume! If we all practised one chapter each week just think what an outstanding leadership team we'd be at the end of the year! Simple and direct advice for all levels of management."
Ian Burnett, Managing Director, Wates Living Space

"There is lots of really insightful and helpful advice in this book. Playing to people's strengths and not wasting time on their weaknesses really hit home to me and made a difference in how I run my business. This book and its power tools are great to dip into. Try it out and watch for the benefits."
Ian Noble, Contract Director, Optimise

"The insightful way, based on first-hand experience, in which Dave Stitt and Paul Fox dismantle the clouds and clutter that construction leaders and their teams create is both refreshing and very helpful. A read that could change the performance of your organisation."
Phil Hughes, MD, PRH Construction Services Ltd.

Contents

Foreword

By Peter Woolliscroft

Leaders change. We grow old and are replaced. But the need for leadership remains and is constantly cited as the reason why project failure occurs.

We hear, "Good leaders are natural leaders. You cannot coach good leadership. Leaders are born and not made."

But those who are led have greater expectations of their leaders than ever before. Our industry is both complex and fragmented and the solutions available are increasing in number all the time.

The major contractor role is yielding to the specialist contractor and manufacturer, who command greater respect and position as the performance of materials creates more options. Decisions become more complex and solutions seldom lie within the scope of any one individual's understanding or experience.

Skilled leaders today must be able to harness the talent around them to drive the best possible solution. They must have a complete understanding of their leadership style and ability if they are to succeed in today's industry.

This book won't turn you into someone you are not. However it sets out very clearly the way leadership skills can help an individual tune their performance to the optimum level, and deliver not just "an ok solution", but the best available.

For those who want to achieve that little bit extra I would highly recommend this book for your reading list.

Professor Peter Woolliscroft is Managing Director of CYNTRA Ltd., London's leading social housing procurement consortium. He is also Chairman of the Strategic Forum for Construction, and a visiting Professor at Northumberland University's School of the Built Environment. Prior to December 2005, Peter was Head of Construction for the Department of Health in England, where he developed the procurement programme, NHS ProCure 21.

Introduction
Construction's massive leadership gap - and how to fill it

We love this industry. I know that sounds stupid. How can you *love* an industry? But we do. It has so many fantastic people doing great things. Speaking for myself, thanks to the people and the opportunities it offered, I went from being a troubled 16-year-old Geordie to a slightly-less troubled respectable guy in a suit driving a BMW. More importantly, I'm as stretched and challenged and exhilarated today as I was when I started.

I love it!

So what we have to say, we say out of affection and respect. It's this: There is a massive leadership gap in construction today.

And it's not just us who are saying it. Top executives tell us: "There's way too much management and not enough leadership." And middle managers tell us: "There's no leadership around here!"

What do they mean?

Take two projects. Each has a poorly understood contract. Each has a design worked up to a roughly equal level of incompleteness - 30%, typically. In each, the right technical skills are assembled, good methodologies, materials, equipment and labour are sourced. Bang goes the starter pistol - and one gallops off to a reasonable finish while the other limps across the line late, over budget, mired in claims, defects and bad blood.

How come? In our view, the answer is leadership.

"Do we go legal?" a customer asks.

We respond: "What result would going legal get you?"

"I know, but we've had enough of these guys. They've been messing us around for two years now."

"Yes, but what result would you get?"

"I just told you."

"Yeah, but I mean what *result* would you *get*?"

There's a silence as the question sinks in. And then comes the exasperated, *"Well what do you suggest?!"*

That silence - it's the sound we make when we're backed into a corner. It's the sound of the leadership gap.

Paul and I have about 50 years in the industry between us and we know how projects start. Perfect strangers with different backgrounds and agendas are thrown together

FIG. 1
Weak, wobbly foundation

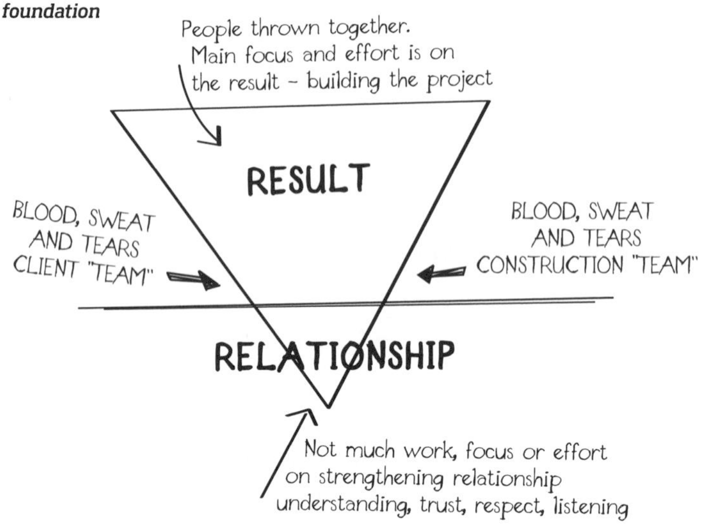

People thrown together.
Main focus and effort is on
the result - building the project

RESULT

BLOOD, SWEAT
AND TEARS
CLIENT "TEAM"

BLOOD, SWEAT
AND TEARS
CONSTRUCTION "TEAM"

RELATIØNSHIP

Not much work, focus or effort
on strengthening relationship
understanding, trust, respect, listening

and expected to deliver huge results.

Most of the time little thought or effort goes into how this motley crew of superb individuals is going to work together. It's just expected that somehow 'natural' leadership will rise to the surface, which is about as realistic as expecting 11 footballers who've never played together and who don't even speak the same language to trot onto the pitch and win the Champions League.

When things go wrong - and things always go wrong - the various parts of the 'team' do everything they've always done, but harder and faster. They throw more time, men and money at the problem. While they're doing that they're retreating into their corners and preparing for the fight. And the result of the fight is two years of heartache and delay and cost and bad feeling.

Have a look at the diagrams. Figure 1 is business as usual. All the focus is on results, with none on relationships. Look at how unstable this huge structure is. And we all know the enormous effort that goes into keeping it up: clients and their teams heaving on one side and contractors and their teams heaving against them on the other.

Figure 2 is how it can be. Care and attention have been given to relationships. Common goals have been identified. Communication is flowing. There is trust, respect, engagement and commitment. In this scenario the project structure is rock solid. It has integrity.

FIG. 2
Stable, strong foundation

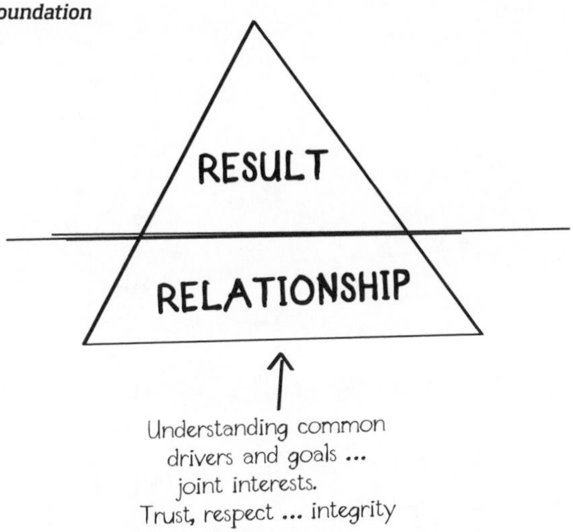

RESULT

RELATIONSHIP

↑

Understanding common
drivers and goals ...
joint interests.
Trust, respect ... integrity

Leadership is about harnessing the massive natural forces embedded in human relationships.

We are amazed at people's reaction when we point this out. Often there is stunned silence as it hits home. Some people say, "Why don't we ever talk about this?" More than a few have said, "Hey, you guys should write a book!"

Challenged and inspired by this, we got busy.

What you have here are reflections on some of the attributes of leadership. Feel free to skip around as the mood takes you. We've kept it short because we know how busy you are - most of the chapters will take 15 minutes or less to read. The power tools are important. They're designed to get you thinking, acting and leading differently, and that's the point!

Have a go and you and your followers will get the most out of this book.

Good luck!

1. The Authentic Leader

WHEN WAS THE LAST TIME YOU SPOKE YOUR TRUTH?

Real leaders are reluctant lemmings. The sheep who like being out of the fold. They've got somewhere better to go and they can take you along.

We once coached the MD of a company who, after a hasty boardroom shuffle, ended up with a director who wasn't really suited to the job. He was a fine and talented person but the company was going through a turbulent time and the role needed a particular set of skills, which he didn't have. We saw it, the MD saw it, the whole executive team saw it, but the MD, fearing more turbulence and also having feelings of loyalty, avoided the problem.

It got awkward. Weeks turned into months. The topic dominated our sessions with the MD, and it got to the point where every conversation he had with his team had a sub-text: *"When are you going to get rid of him?!"*

After six months he grasped the nettle. He called the director into his office, shut the door, laid everything on the table and moved him out. And it was bad. There was real upset. Apart from now having no job, the guy was humiliated. Why didn't you say from the start, he asked? This is what you've all been thinking?

Ouch.

But it worked out well in the end. Soon after he got another job, one in which he's now playing to his strengths and undoubted talent. He's happy and making a difference. And a sense of balance was restored to the MD's team, and the confidence they had in him started to return.

Authentic means 'of undisputed origin', and therefore 'genuine'. It also means 'conforming to reality and therefore worthy of trust, reliance, or belief'. All that is probably no good if you're just shimmying up the greasy pole. Pure boardroom alpinists can't afford to live true to their natures or speak their truths. But for leaders, who need genuine trust and buy-in from their team in order to achieve a difficult result, authenticity is a must.

The first imperative is to be who you are. Be true to your beliefs, your nature, your ambitions, your likes, dislikes and take on the world. Accept your strengths *and* your foibles, weaknesses, and gaps. It's all you. The second is to say out loud the thing that is important and true – as soon as possible after it hits you.

There are two big reasons why leaders need authenticity.

The first is because you, personally, will function more effectively with it. You'll have more power. Why? Because you're working with the tools and perspectives you genuinely possess. It takes far more energy to fake it. In my own experience the more authentic I am the better my results are, the happier I am, the less I struggle, the less stressed I am, the more fun I am to be around, the better are my relationships, the more effective I am and the easier I am on myself. It all just seems to click.

The second reason is that you'll have more magnetism and authority. You won't be just another cardboard-cutout personality. There's a terrible thirst for authenticity out there. Mass media has homogenised all areas of life, from politics and entertainment through to business. Politicians and CEOs alike rig up uniformly safe personae

GET REAL

1. Do The Authenticity Maximiser™
2. Choose one area to be authentic about in the coming month. Tell the people who'll be most affected and ask for their support.
3. Repeat once a month. Notice the response you get, your level of influence and your results. Wear a seatbelt and enjoy the ride!

and stuff us to the gills with apple pie and motherhood. We despise politicians, estate agents, lawyers and journalists because in their various ways they're seen to manipulate the truth, to tell us what we want to hear for their own ends. Hip-high in all this mush it's no wonder we wade toward people who are singular and unique and who tell it like it is.

People pay us, as coaches, to say what we believe. Others aren't so lucky. We work with senior leaders, people you'd think would be comfortable in their own skins, but many ask: 'Who should I be more like?' For 40% of the time leaders hold back when they shouldn't. We didn't just make that figure up. Paul devised a really useful tool called The Authenticity Maximiser™ and the average score arising from dozens of leaders tested in our programmes is about 60%. They're usually shocked by their results.

Why is it so hard?

For many, the urge to 'fit in', to be 'one of the guys', is powerful. We don't want to seem weird, or eccentric – which means, literally, 'situated away from the centre'. But real leaders are by definition eccentric. They're not like everybody else. They're the reluctant lemmings. The sheep who like being out of the fold. They've got somewhere better to go and they can take you along. Leaders we coach often have black moments. 'Am I the only one who gets this?' they ask. Yup. But probably not for long. Keep going.

The other scary thing is that being authentic involves being unpopular sometimes, either with individuals, like our MD above, or with entire factions. But you can't be authentic and liked all the time. There's no surer recipe for getting nothing done than trying to please everybody. Nor can you be authentic and also forever tippy-toeing around everybody's sensibilities. Trying to manage what people think of you is fruitless. Also, it's none of your business. They're as unique and unrepeatable as you and they'll think what they like. When I started doing this job I used to wonder how I could get through the day with everybody still liking me (as if everybody would've liked me from the beginning anyway). I'm pleased to say I'm much better at what I do now.

Note: This is not a free ticket to mouth off, insult, criticise and blame. Say the thing that is important and true but say it with compassion. This takes practice, trial and error. Also be prepared to say you were wrong. No one wants a leader who's wrong all the time but admitting it builds trust.

Timing is key. Say the truth when it hits you. I've learned that the hard way, many times. Once when I was a thrusting young construction manager I switched companies and the first job I helped tender for with the new company was building a warehouse – a big tin shed – which I'd done many times before. In negotiations I said privately to my team that we should price in safety netting for the steelworkers and roofers. It was normal practice at my old company. But our commercial manager said no - we didn't have the £20,000 to spare. At the time it wasn't a legal requirement, but health and safety inspectors very much preferred it. Their attitude was, no, you don't *have* to have netting, but if you don't we're going to count every last band-aid in your first-aid kits. I kept shtum during tendering but after we won I went ahead and put up a net. It was the right thing to do but it caused a big stink. I never got over it with the commercial manager. We never spoke normally again. In meetings we'd sit there stony-faced, furiously blanking each other. All that silly tediousness could have been averted had I spoken my truth when it hit me.

One final thing. Many people are authentic, but leaders should also be *seen* to be authentic. They need to be *vivid*. One way of expressing your authenticity is to tell your stories, even if they expose things you'd rather keep hidden. We're trained to hide mistakes and failure but we should use them strategically to make ourselves real. It's not weakness, it's strength. Look at Barack Obama. In his autobiography he admitted using, as a young man, cocaine and marijuana - and he inhaled. The result? Er, not much. Except that a big skeleton got turfed out of his closet early on.

Vivid stories need light and shade. For thousands of years before DC Comics served up Superman in 1938, all the heroes and gods of old, from the Greek myths to the Norse sagas, were far from squeaky-clean. They sulked, lied, flew off the handle, murdered, plotted revenge, caved in to temptation and screwed up. Traditional heroes weren't 'nice', they were big: all the human characteristics were amplified in them. That's why the stories got passed down for millennia. They matched our inner template of what it is to be human. Being 'flawed' didn't come into it. They were *real*.

The Authenticity Maximiser: How real are you?
Notice to what degree you sell out your unique thoughts and convictions, and consequently your leadership power, integrity and vitality. Be a tough marker. Maximum marks of 100 is a lifelong project

I...	1 = Never 10 = Always
Say what I think and feel without worrying about ridicule or criticism from others	
Am willing to be 100% straight even if others might get upset	
Do what I do because I want to, not because others think I should	
Stand my ground when faced with contention versus habitually caving in or selling out	
Respond with purpose and thought to situations and conflict, versus a knee-jerk reaction when my 'buttons are pushed'	
Stay 'true to myself' versus making me or my viewpoint smaller around people who are 'smarter', 'more senior', 'more charismatic' or more 'pushy' than me	
Get over setbacks quickly versus brooding on regrets or endlessly go over what I could or should have said	
Can say that my words and actions come from conviction about my true value versus proving myself or seeking justification	
Have no trouble admitting I don't know the answer	
Recognise my needs and tell people what I want and how they can satisfy me	

2. The Believable Leader

WOULD YOU RATHER HAVE FOLLOWERS OR BELIEVERS?

Tony's big thing was slyness. He didn't stand for anything apart from business-as-usual. Actually, it was business-as-usual 'deluxe'.

E arly in my career a project I was working on got into trouble and the company had to parachute in a new project director. I'll call him Tony. He was rumoured to be a good trouble-shooter.

I didn't like him. He was guarded and avoided meeting your eye. But he did form a quick bond with one senior member of the team and the two of them were in a permanent huddle. In meetings they had a system of looks and winks.

Tony's big thing was slyness. Despite the difficulties in the project we'd tried to foster straight talking and good relationships but for him it was all psychological chess. The only time he ever warmed up was when he was working up a plan to do over a subcontractor or the client's agent. He also sounded - and I hesitate to say this - thick. He was actually very cunning but he spoke in clichés - 'nose to the grindstone', 'sweeten the pot', etc., and he peppered every sentence with meaningless fillers, like 'at the end of the day', 'ultimately', 'when all is said and done', and that sort of thing. In meetings I used to get angry waiting for some actual content. Later I realised he talked like this because he used empty verbiage to buy time to think. He got a nickname: The Snake.

The job got done. It had the usual number of claims, the usual low margins, the usual level of customer dissatisfaction and, as we packed up for the next job, the usual sour taste lingered in our mouths.

Tony moved on. I don't know where. Later I heard he left the industry in the 1991 recession. But for a long time after that job he fascinated me. In many ways he was utterly normal. By the standards of the time his reputation as a reliable pair of hands was well earned. It was only when I began studying leadership that it dawned on me what rankled me about him: in his professional life Tony had no belief. He didn't stand for anything apart from business-as-usual. If anything, he stood for business-as-usual 'deluxe'. His talent was a kind of negative one. I'm not being naïve. In the 80s and 90s, especially, ruthlessness and sharp practice were expected and rewarded. But it didn't sit well for most and it drove many out of the industry for good. Tony, however, seemed to take to it like a duck to water. He operated at the lowest common denominator and was happy to dip below it.

He made an impression because even during those dark days of the industry I'd had the privilege of working under people who did have real belief. They acted with deliberation according to principles – even if it was at the expense of short-term advantage. Often they were older and remembered when the industry wasn't so fragmented and cut-throat. One in particular lived by the following mantra: 'No excuses, no lies, no surprises.' When I say 'lived by' I mean in his personal life, in dealing with his own team, in dealing with subcontractors, and with clients. If you worked under him you lived by it, too. And it wasn't easy. Unpack it and it has profound implications for the way you behave and the way you think. He was a thoughtful man. Behind the nifty phrase was a lifetime of reflection, trials, errors and omissions.

People with strong beliefs are 'believable' and they exert a powerful influence on a team. Because they stand for values that cut through short-term advantage and shifting self-interest, believable leaders are little beacons of civilisation. Good people gravitate to them. Believable leaders attract, engage and guide talent.

You should be a bit of a bore about your beliefs. They give you a story to tell, so tell it. It allows people to spot you as believable. It lets them get to know what you're about. The ones who like it will stay around and be energised.

Living a principled life may seem hard but it actually makes everything easier. When we know what we stand for it's easier to set a course. If you believe business is better if it's transparent, for instance, and some jiggery-pokery crops up, you don't dither about dealing with it.

I know. This is all very fine and worthy, but where does it leave us in the roller-ball world of business? Should a leader stand by his beliefs even when they put him in conflict with the objectives of his employer? An excellent question! And one I'm heartily relieved to pass on to someone else, the grand-daddy of ethical enquiry, Aristotle.

In his book, *The Nichomachean Ethics*, he developed the idea of 'the mean', meaning the optimum point between two extremes. Take the virtue of courage. He says the kind of courage we should aim for falls somewhere between rashness, as in Charge of the Light Brigade, and cowardice, as in high-tailing it at the sound of the first shot.

But what is that optimum point? Aristotle said it's not an exact science. It will be different for every person and every situation. For those wanting moral absolutes this will sound like a cynical work-around, but Aristotle didn't see it that way. For him, virtue was like horsemanship. You didn't become a skilled horseman by having it accurately described to you. It took a lifetime of practice, commitment, effort and reflection.

Believable leaders tread fine lines in business. If they didn't they'd be priestly hermits and therefore not, by definition, leaders. But believable leaders ask questions like: What will this do to my reputation? How does this colour how my team sees me? What example does this set? What sort of practices and mindsets does it spawn? How am I going to explain this to my wife? And, crucially: Am I prepared to go on earning my living this way?

A quick-fire test: What do you stand for? The clock's ticking. Did your answer emerge clean, crisp and quick? Or was it deer-caught-in-the-headlights time? If it was the latter, you need to a) get clarity on your beliefs, and b) master the language of belief.

THE PRINCIPLES AUDIT

Power tool n°2

1. Identify the big result you and your team are setting out to achieve. (Note: It's okay to copy someone you admire.)
2. Take time out to reflect on what you believe about that result, the challenges for you and your team and whether how you behave matches up.
3. Find someone you trust and who knows the business you're in.
4. Have a go at describing what you believe to your mate and how you will behave as a result.
5. Ask how it sounds. Listen carefully.
6. Convincing? Great.
7. Wishy-washy? False? You'd better check out if those beliefs are real.
8. If they're out of synch, begin adjusting your actions to match your beliefs.
9. Talk about it. Swap "I think..." with "I believe..." - but mean it.

3. The Coach Leader
WHEN WAS THE LAST TIME SHOUTING DELIVERED A GREAT RESULT?

Bully Generation Y and they'll walk, even if it means having to move back in with Mum or Dad. In fact, because property prices are so high (thanks to us), they probably haven't left home yet.

"**D**AVE STITT IS A BASTARD!"

There it was, scrawled on the back of the toilet door. When I saw it I thought, Fantastic! I've landed! In those days just starting out with Taylor Woodrow I felt I had to impress the world, so I ran around shouting at everybody.

And my autocratic, command-and-control style served me well in the 80s. It was expected. Years later when I was at Birse, which was going through a big culture change programme, I learned that grinding down some of my edges actually produced better results. Change was in the air and I was hungry for it. It made some of the guys who knew me uncomfortable. "We used to know where you were coming from Dave," they'd say. "Now you've gone all cuddly."

I don't know what I'd do if I saw that on a wall today. Probably burst into tears.

Anyway, thankfully, the days of 'bark, bollock and bite' are over. There may be a few pockets where it's still the norm, like a lone pterodactyl in the jungles of Borneo, but being shouty and aggressive is not the way of the future.

Two reasons for this.

First, the people you're leading won't stand for it. And here, in case you've not formally met, I'd like to introduce you to 'Generation Y'. This is what self-proclaimed demographic trend-spotters have decided to call people born after December 31st 1981, whose fresh faces you've probably seen in the ranks. Say hello to them. Don't be shy! This is the future - as far as the rest of your career is concerned, anyway.

So what are they like, these Generation Ys? (They're also called 'Millennials'.) Well, apart from looking really young and being rather keen on electronic gadgets, I don't know for sure. I've read some of the literature and the 'findings' were so sweeping and peppered with exceptions that I started to think that trying to label a generation was like selling snake oil. So I'll stick to what I know, from observing a few in work and from what I see in my friends' kids. And what I can report is this: bully them and they'll walk. Even if it means having to move back in with Mum or Dad. In fact, because rents and property prices are so astronomical (thanks to us Baby Boomers) they probably haven't left home yet, so that bit doesn't matter. They'll just go get some other job, or volunteer at an organic farm or start a community project or chill with their 273 Facebook friends.

It drives Baby Boomers like me crazy. Where's their commitment? And why don't they wear ties! But that's the way it is. Broadly speaking, Generation Y haven't known hunger or want. Boomers didn't either, really, but the fear and memory of it was strong in our parents, and it got into us. That's why we cleaned our plates and were grateful for a full-time job with decent prospects and worked all hours and ignored the big questions - What's my life about? How can the planet be a better place for everybody? - and took the abuse, dished out by people like me.

Millennials won't stick at a job if it's demeaning or dull. They don't see why they should. I don't either, frankly.

We're not down on Generation Y. To some Boomers they may seem like spoiled prima donnas. And maybe some are. But we've seen them at work in companies who've made an effort to accommodate them and they're a breath of fresh air. They may have an unrealistic sense of entitlement sometimes, and this may need evening out, but they also have high standards and they bring new sensibilities and skills. They're better educated, better connected and they have a broader emotional range. Paul tells me that the Royal Marines figured this out and are re-writing their whole approach to recruitment and training. These young people come in, maybe from being stockbrokers in the City or some other career. They want to do three years, maybe four - including combat in Afghanistan. They want to achieve excellence in certain things and then they want to move on. While there, they're highly motivated and highly effective.

And they want coaching. Because it works.

Which brings us to the second reason why being shouty and aggressive is backward: compared to a coaching style, it gets inferior results. What you get from bullying is shallower and doesn't last as long.

I say a coaching *style* because we're not asking you to be coaches. Coaching is a rigorous discipline offered by professionals to a growing number of executives who see the benefits of it. But there are elements of coaching you can incorporate into your leadership technique.

Coaching as a discipline emerged in the 70s with pivotal texts like Tim Gallwey's *The Inner Game of Tennis*. He said that when we play tennis (or anything) there are actually two of us out there on the court. Self One is the natural, instinctive part of us stepping up to do the thing without thinking, responding and adapting instantly like the amazing physical creatures we are. Self Two is the parental voice shouting "Straighten up!" "Remember your grip!" "Move forward!" "Relax!" Gallwey watched tennis coaches shouting and decided they just got in the way. So he stepped back. He'd show a video of a brilliant tennis player and say not very much, except maybe "look at the spin on that ball coming over the net" and that sort of thing. Somehow it silences the inner critic. This revolutionised sports psychology and caught on in the arts and professions and business, too.

Here's a tip: coach leaders focus strengths, not weaknesses. They look at what you're brilliant at, make it work better for you, and find workarounds for weaknesses. Delegation, for instance. In most teams one person's weakness is another's strength.

Traditional corporate HR practice hasn't got this yet. Take the annual performance review. I did them for 20 years and most were useless. The author Daniel Pink calls them 'as enjoyable as a toothache and productive as a train wreck'. No matter how you tweak them they still focus on weakness. The boss and you get together, usually with zero preparation, and the boss says 'Okay, you're good at this, but not good at this, that and the other so what shall we do about it?' You don't hear the good, only the bad, so you grimace your way through to some bogus action plan and leave the room feeling hacked off, and everybody forgets about it until the day before the next appraisal. As an exercise it's worse than useless because it de-motivates.

The quest for mastery is a powerful motivator. But your job isn't to oversee a person's overall mastery. That's a personal, lifetime journey. Meanwhile most people have good things to offer right now. The coach leader taps into this talent pool and

RESET YOUR TEAM
ACCORDING TO STRENGTHS

Do a strengths audit

(The opposite of a performance review.) Meet with top team members individually. 20 minutes, max. Ask them which part of their jobs they feel most passionate about and what they feel they're really good at. Listen carefully. Then tell them what you think they're really good at. Listen to their response. Then lay out the results the team must deliver (not the tasks each member must perform) and discuss how the member can best contribute to that. Ideas from you, ideas from them. If there's no immediate convergence, negotiate.

Further handy hint

For quick feedback on your leadership style, do an audit on yourself. Ask five honest colleagues to write three words to describe your leadership, and to fold the paper once. Go round and collect in a hat. (It needs to be like a secret ballot or they won't be honest.) Retire to a quiet spot and read. Don't try and work out who wrote what. Compare, collate and reflect. Ask, is this your most effective leadership style?

Also

Have you thought of using a coach? Coaching has come a long way since the 1970s, and it's now quite common for business leaders to have personal coaches, though they don't always admit it. Coaches aren't counsellors or agony aunts. They help you get clear on the results you want and how to achieve them. Call us to discuss.

harnesses a suite of gifts to accomplish a task. In a project setting, which is temporary, if you focus on their weaknesses it'll be exhausting and the best you can hope for are stronger weaknesses.

The coach leader also appreciates his or her people. To appreciate something is to increase its value. People achieve more when they feel valued. If you have to criticise, pair it with a specific request for what you want. The non-coaching leader will say

'You're useless at that, get your act together', which, for the person on the receiving end, sheds no light on how to improve. Specific requests do the trick.

But, you say, how can I fly with the eagles when I have to work with turkeys? Good question. In his brilliant book *Good to Great*, Jim Collins scoffs at that pious cliché – 'Our people are our greatest asset' – which gets bandied about by directors who'd sooner cross the street than actually talk to a specimen of this great asset. Correction: our greatest asset is our *right* people, and our biggest liability is our *wrong* people. He says we put up with the wrong people for way too long, so get the right people with the right competencies and attitude on board and chuck the rest off the bus, quickly. He's probably right. But the reality is, unless we're starting from scratch and have the money and power to pick and choose from a river teeming with talent, most of us have to work with what we've got. For now. So all the above still applies. Also, before you chuck someone off the bus, do a reality check on your own leadership style. If you're Mr. Shouty Crackers the problem may be you.

Finally, does a coach leader have to be nauseatingly nice all the time? Far from it. Disappointment, exasperation and anger are real feelings and should be expressed. You've got to show steel sometimes. But a coach leader does it strategically, with a specific result in mind, and always with a regard for the other person's dignity and value. (For more on this see "Emotive" and "Unreasonable".)

4. The Confident Leader

ARE YOU WORRYING ABOUT THE SIZE OF THE MOUNTAIN OR ENJOYING THE HIKE?

Your confidence is a rare and delicate garden. You can either cultivate it or let it get choked with rubbish and weeds.

I used to think cash flow was the lifeblood of a business, but now I know it's confidence.

What happens when confidence drains out of a team? Either because times are tough or because of poor leadership? People hesitate. They avoid decisions. They retreat into safe routines. They cover their backs. They sit at their desks waiting for emails to answer instead of getting out there and making things happen. They copy you into every communication. Walk around and they may *appear* busy but there are a thousand ways of filling a day, and many things you can put off until tomorrow - such as making that difficult call to a customer or sticking your neck out with a great idea.

This is a frozen team. The results may not show up right away. Things might seem to be ticking along. But all the while relationships are cooling, market intelligence is not filtering up to you, opportunities are being missed and the stream of work is slowing - all of which saps confidence further.

A lack of confidence is a virulent bug. Remember the 2008 Olympic sprint relays in Beijing? In the qualifying heat the US team, who were seasoned world champions, eliminated themselves spectacularly by dropping the baton. After that the jitters set in and batons were dropping all over the shop in both the men's and women's finals. "Just get the baton round!" the TV commentators were shouting. Right on our screens we could see the whole challenge narrowing down to *mustn't drop the baton!*, and there is no better recipe for baton-dropping.

Fortunately, confidence is highly catchy, too. The fact that the UK were able to win a few early golds meant that team confidence shot up and the British got their biggest medal tally in 100 years.

Leaders can do a lot to pump confidence back into in an organisation, but only if they're confident themselves. One young man we coached was very talented, to the point of being marked out as star material in his organisation, but a lack of confidence was hobbling him on his first big solo flight as project manager. His fright of anything going wrong made him cling to systems and processes, which meant he didn't trust any of the hugely experienced people around him, which got up their noses and made it hard for them to help. With coaching he was able to see what he was doing and start letting go a little. Sure enough, the talent embedded in the whole team was released and things began to flow.

In companies that foster a top-down, command-and-control culture, confidence is treated like the family jewels, cordoned off and kept under guard in the executive wing. Each morning everyone from the tea-person to the operations director queues up outside the CEO's office for instructions.

We see confidence suffer in joint venture situations, like public sector framework agreements. When you get two or more teams thrown together, often with barely an introduction beyond the top-tier personnel, the collision of cultures is rarely pretty. Confidence is usually the first casualty. Nobody takes any decisions and everybody toes their respective party lines, which means nobody tells the truth. In team-building interventions we've done the signs were depressingly common: all communications channelled through one, senior - and therefore insanely busy - individual; written permissions and other bureaucratic controls required for basic activities like site visits; and man-marking, where you watch your opposite number in the other organisation and he watches you.

We've seen grown men, temporarily recalled home from such 'partnerships', actually breaking down and crying with frustration. These guys are supposed to be *on the same side*.

The irony is, when we get them together and spend time defining goals the two teams invariably come up with exactly the same things. But without the lubricant of confidence the machine grinds to a halt.

In one situation we lobbied for, and finally got, agreement from the bosses of both organisations to hold a joint workshop entitled 'Moving Forward With Confidence'. Sixty people from the two sides were keen to take part. But the higher-ups were nervous. Who knew what cans of worms might get opened? It was called off, then put back on again, then the date changed a few times until, finally, an email came through from on high. *'Moving Forward With Confidence has been permanently cancelled'*, it said.

Confidence rubs off on others. Work alongside someone who has purpose and confidence and you feel it too. But how do you get it if you're at the top?

I think of confidence as a marvellous but delicate garden. We've all got one, but for many of us it's neglected and choked with weeds. Just like an actual garden, you have to do lots of things to tend and nurture it. Everybody's different, but here are the top things on my job list for confidence cultivation.

1. Exercise every day. Something enjoyable: walking, running, cycling, squash, tennis, chopping wood - whatever. It reboots your hard drive and releases endorphins. Also, when you feel fit, you feel confident.
2. Spend time with excellent people. It might be a neighbour, a friend, a colleague, a customer, a partner or a child. Excellent people inspire, challenge and support. They get you out of yourself, broaden your perspective, make you laugh and feel better.
3. Develop and share your unique abilities. Everyone's brilliant at something. Your experience, knowledge, upbringing and natural talents form an unrepeatable composite. Identify, develop and share these gifts. The feedback works wonders.
4. Appreciate your team. I mean the way you would an asset, as in, increase its value. You can appreciate your team (in both senses of the word) by acknowledging their talents and achievements regularly. Just watch their stock rise.
5. Get money in the bank. Yes, you do need cash, so make sure you invoice and get paid on time.
6. Build relationships with customers. Relationships are the foundation for everything, and big results require big relationships. Customers need to be appreciated like anybody else, and so do their businesses.
7. Appreciate your best opportunities. Every day, look at your top five opportunities, and do something to increase their likelihood of happening.
8. Appreciate your own achievements. Make sure you achieve something every day. It might be small, like making a phone call instead of putting it off. Write them down. Every week look back and list the top ten. Do the same every quarter. Confidence is

having the feeling that you're getting somewhere good, and it helps to stop and see how far you've come. You can do this with your team, too.

9. Work on a health plan. I've decided I'm going to be healthier and fitter in 20 years than I am now. I can honestly say I'm approaching 50 fitter than I was at 40. It's a fantastic feeling, and it makes me feel confident.

10. Be straight with everybody, especially yourself. If it doesn't come out right, get straight back in and apologise. It's hard, but being honest will make you feel better, lighter, clearer and more confident. Don't sugar-coat bad news for your team. When things are bad, they know. What they need is the truth, so they can do what they need to do to manage.

I work on at least one of these every day and it's a habit now. You may have different confidence boosters. Write them down and work on them.

Finally, you can't have confidence without action. When you're landed with a horrible situation, or when a huge, unpleasant task looms, the temptation is to sit, worrying and brooding about what a vast, ugly mountain you've got to climb. Sometimes you're frozen there for ages, looking at the mountain and shaking your head. But hopefully at some point you step forward, grab the first hand-hold and hoist yourself up – and your whole perspective changes. Confidence and 'oomph' start flowing back in. Soon you've forgotten all about the mountain and you're just throwing yourself at the task. This goes for individuals and teams. Pick up the phone. Start a conversation. Get people in a room. You don't have to map everything out first, just get moving.

Remember, when confidence is high, the only limit to what you can achieve is what you conceive – what you can *think up*. When confidence is low all you can do is defend, retreat and ultimately exit the field.

THE TEAM THAW

`Power tool n° 4`

1. Assemble team in a room.
2. Have them list their concerns, every last one of them.
3. Red line the ones you can't influence, like the economy, a competitor's stroke of luck, legislation, acts of God, etc.
4. Green underline the ones you can influence.
5. Pick the top five 'greens' and identify the first action you can take for each. (Important: Don't try and 'solve' each of these five, just come up with the first step. The rest will flow naturally later.)
6. Assign responsibility for each action, set a deadline and a report-by date.
7. Repeat as necessary.

This simple exercise has a remarkable effect. I've seen people drag themselves in, full of gloom, and leave with a bounce in their step and chatting excitedly. Having a plan and getting on with it brings confidence flooding back in.

Thanks to Shannon Waller at Strategic Coach for the inspiration and the practical exercise. Visit: www.strageticcoach.com

5. The Connected Leader
ARE YOU COMMUNICATING OR JUST TRANSMITTING?

Chronic disconnection turns potential leaders into ineffective bystanders. It ruins opportunities to influence and engenders bad feeling.

Keith, my business manager, tells me his eyes glaze over the minute I go into 'transmit mode'. He's so right. An idea comes to me in the car and I've only got 10 minutes before I get to the meeting or wherever I'm going, so I call him up, pretend to be friendly and relaxed, and say, "Hey Keith, there's something I need to run by you but I've only got 10 minutes. Is that okay?"

He knows what I really mean is: "Can I dump everything in my head into yours and can you not interrupt or say anything or even breathe until I decide I've had enough and need to go?"

"Sure," he says.

At which point I commence transmitting. And he carries on doing whatever he was doing before, with me droning on in the background, biding his time for a real opportunity to communicate. He told me he actually put me on hold once, went to another line, ordered a curry, and came back on the line without me noticing.

A leader's job is to get a group of people to step out of the ordinary, to be more than the sum of its parts, and you can't do that unless you connect with them. You may have oodles of experience, a flawless track record and brilliant ideas. You may also be a brilliant 'communicator' (i.e., a brilliant transmitter). Your speeches and letters should maybe even be recorded for posterity, they're so good. But in the ordinary world of people and business and action, connection is *the* currency of loyalty, unstoppable commitment and engagement. Without it you'll never get any real traction with people and your influence will be superficial.

Why? I don't know. It's a mystery. For some reason connection is as vital for us as food is, or water. Babies deprived of it fail to thrive. For special punishment prisoners get bunged in solitary confinement, which some people want banned as a form of psychological torture. I spend a lot of time out talking to people and doing workshops and during longer stretches of working in my office I get bored, depressed and aimless without even realising it. Then I pick up the phone and talk to somebody and my mood lifts miraculously.

In his book *The Fifth Discipline Fieldbook,* Peter Senge notes that among the tribes of northern Natal the most common greeting is "sawu bona" which means "I see you". If you're a member of the tribe you say "sikhona", or "I am here". It's as if you don't actually exist until you're seen.

In hostage situations, according to expert negotiator Stuart Diamond, when the bad guys demand food, clever negotiators don't deliver trays of sandwiches. They send in loaves of bread, cheese, ham, and jars of condiments. Why? Because it forces the bad guys to make lunch for their hostages, which sparks connection with them, which makes it that little bit harder to kill them.

We do our best for people we connect with. We just do. And it's because we want to. Sticks and carrots are not required. That's because when we connect with somebody they become real to us and we become real to them. Suddenly, they *matter.* Our systems and values kick into life. We bring our whole selves to bear on the transaction, whatever the transaction is. We move from lip service to a full-throated exchange.

How can you tell if you're not connecting? A sure sign is that you're fed up, bored and exhausted. You're struggling to get others to do what you want, to raise their game, see the bigger picture, accomplish more, maybe even buy your service or product. You've tried persuading, instructing, provoking, entertaining and manipulating, but nothing shifts. If that's you, you may have mistaken transmission for connection.

Chronic disconnection has serious results. For one thing it turns potential leaders into ineffective bystanders. We see managers who do the obligatory visit to the problem job, only to squeeze off a few platitudes in the site manager's cabin and vanish without having either made or taken away impressions of any worth. Their opportunity to influence is lost.

For another, it breeds bad feeling. While he was a regional director for a national contractor one of our associates recalls being teamed up with a director from another region. They failed to connect. This other guy was so polished and pleasant that an exchange with him left about as much trace as a piece of candy floss. "You slipped off him like Teflon," our associate said. He admits his reaction was not very grown up. "We just started building separate empires. It made me feel mischievous. I'd nick work off him whenever I could. It was bad for business."

Is it any wonder? If you don't connect, or worse, if you actively resist connection with someone who reaches out because of work or some other circumstance, you're actually stopping that person becoming *real*. It amounts to an existential snub. You're 'blanking' them. How do we feel when we're blanked? Put-off, at least. Resentful. Angry even. Humiliated. I remember we had a new MD once who was doing the rounds and he said "Stitt, we need to talk." I was thrilled, but then he never followed up so my attitude soured to "Sod you, then".

The good news is there is simple stuff you can do to connect better. Here is our 12-point plan for connecting better with the people who matter:

1. Don't email. It's pure transmission, self-publishing, speechifying, whatever, anything but connection. (Oh, the amount of time I've wasted getting my dander up in an email, to zero effect.)
2. Make a call. The give and take of a real, live conversation, even over the phone, is probably the minimum you need to get some connection going.
3. Go visit. Get in the person's actual presence. If you need to be real to somebody, go be real.
4. Make eye contact. Be there. Don't check your Blackberry, stifle a yawn or send any one of a thousand other signals that you're actually somewhere else.
5. Empty your mind of noise and distraction and really listen to what they say, and to what you're saying.
6. Tell them you're listening. Nod your head encouragingly. Give them prompts. (Women do this better then men, I find.) Say stuff like 'Uh huh', 'Yes', 'No! Really?' 'So that means...', etcetera. This works.
7. Learn something every time. Everyone has hidden depths they'd love to reveal. Make it your mission to find out something new about the person whenever you interact.

8. Lead with questions, not answers. Ask more questions than you receive - nice, open, leading questions. The manager will get way more out of the site visit by having a few of these to hand, like 'What should I know?' 'Tell me something I don't want to hear.' 'Tell me something great about the last few days.'

9. Show your vulnerability. It's okay to admit mistakes and to not knowing the answer. It makes for way more interesting conversations.

10. Show up as a human being first and MD or whatever second. People buy into you first, not your title.

11. If you want to find out something more real, of substance, about another person, share something real, of substance, about yourself.

12. Admit defeat. It's true that some people are just impossible to connect with. If you're sure you've given it your best shot, accept it and think again about what's really possible in that relationship.

Remember, you don't have to put on some 'life-and-soul-of-the-party' mask. Shy people can connect, too. We worked with the chief executive of one well-known firm who was painfully shy but who got a lot of mileage out of just explaining once in a while to people that he didn't feel comfortable with strangers or standing up in front of groups. Admitting that made him understandable, and therefore real.

DO A 'BILL CLINTON'

Power tool n° 5

The former US president was rumoured to be a legendary connector. It's said that in conversation with him you got the feeling he was with you and nowhere else. There are limits, of course, to the level of connection appropriate in a work setting, but with that in mind why not try some of the old Clinton magic? Identify three people you really need better connection with and shake up your usual stale communications with the tips above. Notice how your 'bandwidth' increases, and how much more traction and engagement you get.

Further reading: Since it was first published in 1937, I don't think anybody has actually improved on Dale Carnegie's *How to Win Friends and Influence People*.

Also, think of your customers. The world is more dehumanised than ever with all the automated systems, synthetic human voices, blaring ads and websites, and so on. The flipside is that the smallest show of humanness packs loads of punch. This can mean anything from hand-writing letters and being interested in who they actually are, to exposing them to your front line troops as opposed to just the slick frontmen. Humanise your customer's experience and you stand out a mile.

And don't fear sparks! Connection doesn't always mean 'nice'. If a relationship is difficult or messy it doesn't mean connection isn't possible. That's often where the greatest potential for connection lies. Real relationships *are* messy. People are annoying when you get to know them. But the alternative, arranging life so we avoid discomfort

Cautionary tale - the seductive power of connection
One of our associates had been seconded as a management consultant to a manufacturing firm. This story about the MD of that firm, a guy we'll call Henry, shows the sometimes distorting power of connection.

"I'd never seen anybody like Henry before," our associate recalls. "He talked to everybody on the floor. He knew the names and birthdays of everybody's wife or husband, who'd had a new baby, who'd had a new puppy, the lot. He wasn't particularly funny or slick or a big personality, he was just so there. His management team, especially the production guys, would have followed him into the mouth of Hell. One day he said he was leaving. It was actually during a weekend training programme. He dropped the bomb at dinner on the Saturday night, saying it was time he moved on, that he couldn't achieve his goals with this company, etcetera. We didn't buy it. We were convinced he'd been given the shove. It was chaos. We vowed to go with him. We stayed up late and made long, rambling speeches. The next day was a write-off. We didn't finish the course, just sat around with our heads in our hands. But there was nothing we could do. He left.

And then in the weeks that followed it emerged what a terrible MD he'd been. The market had been changing but Henry hadn't been changing with it. He'd had his head stuck in the sand and the business was going down the tubes. We hadn't seen any of that. We believed in the guy."

altogether, means living at such a superficial level that we never push the edges and grow. Conflict is the natural result of deepening connection. The trick is being able to draw out 'dangerous' issues and invite discussion from a position of mutual interest, without everybody flying off the handle.

6. The Disruptive Leader

A manager's job is to solve problems. A leader's, to create them.

Disrupt - *verb*: To prevent something, especially a system, process or event, from continuing as usual or as expected.

Superb definition!

In *The Evolution of Civilizations* historian Carroll Quigley mapped out how civilisations rise and fall. Basically they're born fighting, succeed, get comfy, stagnate and fall apart. I'm condensing loads but that's more or less it. And I think the same holds for just about anything - institutions, companies, products, systems of thought, bands and football teams.

Sounds a bit gloomy, doesn't it? But wait. Quigley also found that civilisations can prolong themselves by dramatic innovations which confound the rules of the game and give them a sudden decisive edge against competing civilisations.

And herein lies one of the main differences between a manager and a leader. Managers are stewards, preserving and fine-tuning systems, while leaders strategically disrupt systems and sail resolutely into the ca-ca storm.

A few years ago a coaching client of Paul's, an MD of an architecture practice, decided the firm should become a significant player in the education sector. Fine in theory, except that nobody had any experience or understanding of that sector. It caused a big problem, not least for the staff who wanted to focus their efforts on the rich supply of commercial development work available then. There was deep resistance. The feeling was that this was a spanner in the works from out of the blue, a solution to a totally imaginary problem. But the MD persevered. They eventually became a leading practice in the education sector and when the bottom fell out of the commercial market in 2008 they were cushioned from the fall.

For many of us, creating problems is counterintuitive. We're taught to prevent problems, fix them or get rid of the people causing them. Usually it's our problem-solving skills that got us to a leadership position in the first place, especially for technical people like engineers and designers. If a client wants a bridge, you don't dredge the river deeper.

Nevertheless, when you look at the big leaps forward you'll find they were often preceded by a problem. In 1908 Henry Ford gave his company a big problem. He said they'd make it possible for most households in the US to buy a car. This was at a time when only 2% of the population could afford one. A car cost $1,500 and the average annual income was $750. In 1908 he launched the Model T for $850. Not a bad start. But thanks to the assembly line by 1924 he'd got the cost down to $290 and more than 60% of households had a Model-T in the drive.

Leaders can cause big problems or little problems. They can be disruptive about anything: external company strategy, internal systems, politics and culture, even the way a particular project is executed.

The MD of one our clients decided to change his company from the traditional regional structure to one based on customer sectors - industrial, civils, education, health care... Imagine the uproar! Fiefdoms got snatched away from under noses, clans and tribes were dispersed and for a while nobody knew who their bosses were. But it worked. Suddenly the knowledge and expertise embedded like needles in haystacks throughout the regions could be mustered to delight any client, anywhere.

Before a 'disruptive environment' can be created, leaders have to be comfortable with chaos and bad feeling. Change and innovation are chaotic. People naturally tend toward paths of least resistance. We work hard for our comfort zones. Individuals do it and organisations do it too. Clients say to us, yeah, we need change, but how do we do it without it getting messy and out of hand? You can't. You can avoid ambiguity and chaos but only by inviting stagnation and decay.

There is no prescribed way of going about a big disruption. We've seen company leaders suddenly announce a new course, get a few hardies on board and manage the fall-out as it happens. We've seen others painstakingly erect a ground-up 'change management' programme to try and minimise the chaos. Each way has its advantages and suits different situations, people and cultures.

Now, it's important to stress that we're not talking about disruption for its own sake. It's not true that anything that disrupts is good. Successful leaders choose their disruptions carefully, and only because they've seen something others don't see or pretend they don't see because it scares them. It's fair to say that when it comes to the big, corporate disruptions most successful leaders might chalk up two, maybe three in their careers.

But how do you choose your problem? This is not really something you can learn in a book. In the examples we've given here the leaders spotted a problem way off on the horizon and brought it right into their organisations and made it real, right now. It was based on hunch, vision, intuition, call it what you will - they picked a direction without the sort of evidence most of us would normally demand. To do it successfully you need to unclutter your mind, climb up on a ridge somehow to gain a perspective others don't have.

We live in a world of accelerating change, which creates both huge breakthroughs in performance and massive uncertainty. One thing is certain: if you're not creating your problems someone else will, and you'll be reacting to those problems on someone else's terms.

ON CAUSING STINKS

`Power tool n°6`

1. Start consciously reducing the time you spend solving problems to balance it out with causing strategic problems.
2. Know when to be stubborn and when to be flexible. Be stubborn on big things, and flexible on little things.
3. Don't change your strategy because certain audiences protest or don't get it.
4. Be willing to fail, be willing to think long-term, and be willing to be disliked for long periods of time. If you can't, stick to management, which is fine - we need good managers just as much as we need good leaders.
5. Now, reflect on and write down the one most pressing change you and your team need to bring about - and go for it!

Further thought: Disruptive leadership can work in your personal life, too.

7. The Easy Leader
WHOEVER SAID WORK HAD TO BE HARD?

Easy places to work are instantly recognisable. Goals are clear, information flows fast to where it's needed, and recognition flows to where it's due. People take pride in their work and enjoy themselves.

Unfortunately, this is a real story.

We were three weeks from handover on a big luxury apartment complex and the taps didn't work. They didn't work because they were designed for a pressurised system and the system we'd put in wasn't pressurised. A meeting was called. Attending, in hierarchical order, were the client, the client's project manager, the architect, the contractor (us) and the services consultant. The project manager, feeling it his duty, strutted around like a rooster demanding to know whose fault it was. We played ping pong with that for half an hour until the ball rolled into the services consultant's corner, where it stayed. Because he was at the bottom of the food chain.

"Right," said the project manager. "You put those taps in. It's down to you."

The MD of this firm was absolutely fuming but said nothing. However at the next meeting, a week later, he came in with a dossier five inches thick, which he thumped on the table and started reciting from start to finish. It took quite a while but he wouldn't be diverted. This dossier proved beyond doubt that the taps he'd put in were the ones the architect had specified, so it wasn't his fault, it was the architect's. He'd had his whole team compiling that dossier all week.

The architect started to argue. Then somebody asked, "Does anybody know how to fix this problem?" After a few seconds a site foreman raised his hand, cleared his throat and said: "Uh, yeah, we've seen this before. If you remove the washers from the taps they work okay."

So we did. And they worked, but not in time to prevent two hours of meetings, a whole week of expensive effort and immeasurable amounts of goodwill from going down the drain.

This is just one small example of the sort of widespread and needless dysfunction that turns our hair grey, bursts our gaskets, drives us to drink and generally makes work - *hard*.

Good leaders, however, create situations where work is easy. How? We asked a group of construction people to list the top three things that makes their boss easy to work for. Normally, getting people to respond is like pulling teeth, but this really struck a chord. We analysed the responses and arrived at the top 10 characteristics of easy leaders. Basically, 'Easy' leaders:

1. Are convincing
2. Allow failure and see it as a chance to develop (in themselves, too)
3. Provide clear feedback on performance
4. Have experience and ability that you respect
5. Have attractive vision and values
6. Let you get on with it and don't muscle into your detail
7. Are available when you need them by phone, email or in person
8. Know what they want and ask for it
9. Are open about what they're thinking and feeling, so there's no need to guess what's going on in their heads
10. Offer recognition

We see some great, easy leaders, and some that are hard work and into struggle and strife. In one company we worked with the MD wrote a number on the flipchart and said 'we can do that'. Three years later that was their turnover. In another the CEO thumped the table and shouted and said everybody had to improve the bottom line or they'd be for the high jump. Three years later the business still had a 1% margin, loads of struggle, acrimony, sudden management departures, factions, arse-covering and a few bad projects dragging down the good ones.

Organisations, and individual projects too, reflect their leadership. You set the tone, and the way you treat people gets replicated - the good bits and the bad bits. As they say, a fish rots from the head.

Easy places to work are instantly recognisable. The organisation's goals are clear and make sense. Information flows fast to where it's needed, and recognition flows to where it's due. People take pride in their work and enjoy themselves. Equally, we can all spot a dysfunctional organisation or project. Its goals are murky or out of synch with what people are actually doing. Information is doled out carefully. Hierarchies are rigid and fiercely protected. Recognition is diverted up to the visible few and the hungry wolf of blame stalks the land.

Forty years ago a psychologist called Mihaly Csikszentmihalyi, a Hungarian-born refugee from Nazi Europe who escaped to America, began studying the mental state of rock climbers, musicians, painters, children, cabinet-makers, anybody who gets so ecstatically absorbed in what they're doing that they forget time, hunger, fatigue, calls of nature and just keep going until they drop. This state, he said, was *flow*. He thought it was great and set out to define it. He noticed that certain things came into play when you're in flow, including:

1. A sense of personal control
2. Challenge, but not too much (it's not too easy or too hard)
3. The activity is intrinsically rewarding (you're doing it for its own sake)
4. Feedback on success or failure comes fast so you can adjust efforts on the hoof

"Every action, movement, and thought follows inevitably from the previous one, like playing jazz," Csikszentmihalyi said in an interview with *Wired* magazine. "Your whole being is involved, and you're using your skills to the utmost."

Most of us get flow sometimes in work or play. Deprived of it, Csikszentmihalyi found, we show signs of mental ill-health. We feel bored, anxious, worried and apathetic. What he and others have begun to ask is, how can we organise our companies so that the opportunities for flow are maximised? So that people are accomplishing great stuff *and* enjoying themselves? So that the line between 'work' and 'play' gets blurry?

I believe industries like construction, where people from various disciplines are thrown together to create something, are more flow-friendly than others. At least I

THE EASY LEADER DIAGNOSTIC   Power tool n°7

1. **Have a look in the mirror. Score yourself as a leader on the 10 characteristics above.**
2. **Ask a few people you trust – for being honest, that is – to score you and discuss how you and them can both make things easier. (Ouch! Be brave...)**
3. **Don't assume things will get any easier unless you do first.**

Further handy hints

Hold a 'surgery': Schedule two hours a week where your door is open and anybody from your team can come in and discuss what's on their minds. In construction, project-specific stuff usually gets dealt with as it arises but deeper issues to do with company strategy, career development or team relations always get put off to a mythical 'later'. This could be a great barometer for your own performance as a leader, too. (Thanks to Daniel Pink, author of *Drive: The Surprising Truth About What Motivates Us* for the idea.)

can't think of many others where the levels of passion, excitement and engagement are so high and widespread. Long days fly past. Which is absolutely great. But I see a lot of flow-inhibiting factors too, like in the story above, and where outmoded, command-and-control styles of management persist.

Being an easy leader ain't easy. It takes practice and thought and trial and error. Looking at the top 10 characteristics confirms what I've known for years - I'm mighty hard to work for, and I definitely hold back the people potential in my business. I score myself five out of 10. I think I'm pretty good at:

- Being convincing. (My colleagues might say there's a fine line between 'convincing' and 'domineering'.)
- Vision and values. My team and I share a passion for being straight, doing a great job, learning and valuing ourselves and our families
- Being open about what I'm thinking and feeling. (Though 'forever banging on' may be more accurate.)

The many things I need to work on include:

- Seeing failure as development. I understand the words but I care so much for our customers and reputation that screw-ups weigh heavily on my mind.
- Being hands off and letting people get on with it.
- Being available. I'm often too busy meddling ('sorting stuff out') to be available.

So being an easy leader is really hard. It's a mastery thing. But it's worth the effort. You can't be a leader unless you have followers, and if you're hard to follow they won't. Not really. They'll submit to being policed and pushed, which turns you into a hard leader, which creates a vicious circle.

8. The Emotional Leader

EMOTIONS STILL RULE. ARE YOU IN THERE RULING WITH THEM?

We're afraid of 'real' conversations because of the emotions they might unleash. But we should be even more afraid of 'unreal' conversations because all they do is kick dirt over smouldering fuses.

You've heard the one about the farmer who sets off across the fields to borrow a tractor from his neighbour? Halfway there he remembers he hasn't returned the cement mixer he borrowed the winter before. Nor did he ever return that bridle he borrowed for his daughter, which he hasn't actually seen for years. It starts to bother him.

'Tough,' he thinks. 'It's harvest time and I need the tractor. And anyway, look at all the times I've helped him out – that time he was short on feed. Or when I interrupted my Christmas lunch to help him round up those sheep. But he won't remember that, will he? Oh no.'

And he pictures his neighbour on the last market day. A certain… off-handedness. Yes, definitely off-hand. Because of the cement mixer, no doubt. And the stupid bridle. And it dawns on the farmer what a selfish, sanctimonious old windbag his neighbour actually is. He arrives and raps on the door. The neighbour opens it and smiles, but before he can say anything the farmer shouts: "*And you know what you can do with your tractor!*'

This story makes me chuckle a) because it rings true and b) because it illustrates the power - the often distorting power - of emotions.

Traditionally in business we don't 'do' emotions. Tears are embarrassing. What's our officially-sanctioned display of grief? A minute's silence, and even that's awkward. On the other end of the spectrum, too much enthusiasm is unseemly, and 'touchy-feely' gives us the creeps. 'Yes, we do want a workshop,' clients tell us. 'But no tree-hugging or anything.'

Our distrust is understandable. Strong emotion can lead to rupture or even violence and situations we feel we can't recover from. And cool heads and stiff upper lips have seen us through many national crises. But too much buttoned-up-ness stifles and can even derail a project or a company vision. We only know a tiny proportion of all there is to know about our brains, but one thing is certain: despite the premium we place on intellect and rationality, emotions still rule. The generations coming after the Boomers are far more in touch with their feelings, and unless you can engage on that level you can't engage at all. 'Emotional intelligence', or 'emotional fluency' is a crucial tool for fostering honesty, commitment, engagement and accountability in a team.

Sometimes in workshops it's necessary to shock people into talking about their emotions. They clearly have something to say but they're holding back. They don't want to speak until they've thought it through. They're 'intellectualising', which means they're taking an angle-grinder to any edges that might either display or spark feeling. Our job is to stop this careful dance around emotions. We disrupt reasonableness. Until they're shaken out of their comfort zone, they won't say anything real. We provoke until they shoot from the hip, which is when the real issue emerges and we can make progress. Until then, we're just wading through treacle.

We're afraid of 'real' - as in 'difficult' - conversations because of the emotions they might unleash: anger, disappointment, blame, etc. But we should be even more afraid of all the 'unreal' conversations we have because all they do is kick dirt over smouldering fuses. It's like trying to tape a lid onto a pressure cooker. In workshops people often want to know how to deal with an issue without it getting 'difficult'. You can't. If we avoid the difficult part we just go round in circles because the place we're trying to avoid is the very place we need to go before we can go anywhere else.

A great example of this came in a workshop we did for a Building Schools for the Future partnership that was going wrong. We'd managed to get the school staff involved and in the charged atmosphere one project leader on the delivery side blurted out that there was no way the project would be complete by the deadline. Silence fell.

This was definitely *not* the party line. The headteacher took a breath and said: "Thank you. That's the first time anybody's admitted that in two years."

What happens when an issue is left to fester between two people? Energy stops flowing between them. They may seem to get along but the walls have gone up. Resentments build. Each amplifies the faults of the other. Privately, each lays blame and builds their case, often without regard to the original facts. Eventually they go their separate ways with bad feeling or it erupts in a blazing row over something trivial. In a team or a company the results are less dramatic but just as damaging. People retreat into enclaves, undermine others and evade responsibility.

Getting past reasonableness is a real breakthrough. One client we coached was the most rational, level-headed person you could meet, so reserved he made Sergeant Wilson off Dad's Army look like a screaming banshee. The problem was, not everybody he dealt with was as reasonable or correct as him. For over a year we tried to help him express himself more.

Finally, he swore at someone. His secretary couldn't believe it. I don't recommend swearing at people but for our client this was a major advance. The guy on the receiving end had frustrated him for years. After the smoke cleared they sorted the issue out. (He also added a new arrow to his communication quiver. If you're reasonable most of the time people do tend to notice when you get excited. He'd broadened his range – increased his *fluency*.)

Being 'emotionally intelligent' means being able to have difficult conversations with skill and compassion, without them causing permanent rupture. That means we have to understand our own feelings and be able to express them accurately. But that's only part of it. We also need to understand how what we do makes others feel and to allow them to express it without fear of counter-attack. Feelings that get expressed – and acknowledged – lose their destructive potency. Your mind clears, your understanding of the situation deepens and empathy and trust are allowed back in.

Note: It's not emotionally intelligent to shout "You're an idiot!" whenever you feel like it. It's not a sanction for wrath and abuse. The point is not to punish or take revenge. What you should say is: "I felt really disappointed and let down when you did that because..."

Becoming more emotionally intelligent is not about 'giving in' to emotions, either. In fact the more emotionally intelligent you become, the less you are ruled by emotions. Expressing them defuses them. They're less likely to force a reaction. There will always be things that push our buttons. The trick is to feel, express, understand and move on. We decide how to feel. Is a setback really the end of the world or a chance to take stock and start again? It's up to us.

Emotions are valuable guides, too. Our clients often face painful decisions. They may know deep down they've got to let someone go, for instance. It might seem wrong theoretically but emotionally they know it's right. They can't help asking what we think. We can't answer but when we turn the question back on them they normally arrive again at what they emotionally 'knew' already. They just needed to let their emotions filter through. There are no definitive right or wrong answers to these questions but decisions based on what you feel is right are far less likely to be wrong. If, conversely, we go against our instincts, perhaps to conform to perceived expectations, we often get burnt - particularly if we find we've sold out when there was no expectation to in the first place.

It's strange that emotional issues are called 'soft issues' in HR parlance, as if they're less crucial than contracts and spreadsheets. The fact is, 'soft' issues can determine the success or failure of a project as much as 'hard' ones.

What's needed right now? Foster emotional intelligence in your team. Start 'doing emotions', because they're as much a part of us as a hand or a leg. Identify them. Talk about them. Use them. Encourage difficult conversations as soon as an issue crops up. They provide intelligence about the team's emotional take on the plan. You start, and be prepared to learn from others because they may be better at it.

EXPRESS YOURSELF!

Most of us have been trained to thrash emotions into submission and squeeze them out of everyday business life. It doesn't work. They come back, disguised as sneaky and low-level emotions like smugness and indignation. Effective leaders work on their 'emotional fluency'. Here's how to start:

1. For a whole week, drop the phrase "I think that..." and swap it with "I feel that..." Be sure to tell the truth, and pay attention to what comes out. (It will get easier.)

2. When you're talking to colleagues, instead of asking "What do you think about that?" ask "How do you feel about that?" If they evade, say how you feel about it and ask again. And again.

9. The Energetic Leader
ARE YOU RUNNING ON FUMES?

Burn-out is awful. You can see where you're supposed to be going but you're stuck in a lay-by with an empty tank.

another typical monthly budget meeting

The second most craved thing among the executives we coach is energy.

(The first is time. Rush on over to that chapter if you must, but come straight back because 'time management' is old hat. The most effective people nowadays are into energy management.)

I used to think my energy levels were beyond my control, that it was all just how I felt on the day. Something 'good' would happen and I'd be on top of the world, then something 'bad' would happen – bad news, bad feedback – and I'd be on the floor.

But I was wrong. We have an abundant source of energy, we just need to know how to use it. Unlike time, it's also a renewable resource. Actually it's better than renewable, because the more you use the more you get.

And what do you get when you run out of energy? Burn-out. Burn-out is awful. Burned out people can still see the vision, all too well, but it fills them with bitterness because they're stuck in a lay-by with an empty tank.

We really like talking about energy because there's stuff you can do, right away, to crank open the energy valves. But first we need to clear something up. People think energy is just a physical thing. In fact, as the author Jim Loehr brilliantly points out, we have four types at our disposal: Spiritual, Emotional, Mental and Physical.

Spiritual energy

This is about having a sense of purpose and knowing where you're going, both at a Life level and day by day. An over-arching Life Purpose is a very personal thing and people who have one are lucky. I'm not qualified to comment on what makes a good one or a bad one. Not here, anyway. Mine's probably best characterised as a 'work in progress', though it fills me with energy and optimism. I will, however, stick my neck out and say that people live richer lives if they at least put some serious thought into it.

Below Life Purpose comes important sub-purposes that should feed into and support your Life Purpose. Work is a biggy, and your sense of purpose in work is a key source of spiritual energy in work. I'm lucky. Mine is to have a successful business that creates real value for customers by doing what I love doing. Cheesy, I know, but it's had me leaping out of bed for 10 years now and I'd be absolutely gutted if I had to stop.

Spiritual energy is a powerful force if you harness it right. In this industry, the traditional font of binding energy has been the war-like sense of us-and-them, small groups of like minded men battling against all comers to win the job and turn a meagre profit from it. Looking back, I'm not immune to a sense of nostalgia for the thrills and camaraderie of that time. Sometimes you can even forget the personal toll it took. But it isn't sustainable. These days you can't expect incoming talent to buy into that vision or accept it as the ultimate reward. Today's 20 and 30-somethings demand a sense of purpose.

Do you have a sense of purpose with work? I mean, a good, meaty one? How does it compare to when you started out in your career? Maybe then what drove you on was getting qualified. Then it was moving up the ladder to become a leader. So you've arrived: what next? Survive another year in business? Does that energise you and your people?

If you don't have a sense of purpose in work, you need to get one. It's a priority. Check out "Inspired" for more on this, or call us for some coaching.

Emotional energy

This is how we're *feeling*. Emotional energy determines the *quality* of our energy. So if you're hacked off with the world your energy is heavy and negative and drags everybody down. You can work on this, and I don't mean forcing yourself to be 'positive'. There are practical things you can do to make yourself happier and you have a responsibility to do them.

One way is to sort out issues with people straight away rather than letting things fester. Years ago a coach had me make a list of all the people I had an issue with, and all the people I thought had an issue with me, and I spent *two years* going through that list and making things right as best I could. There were some really great conversations and some really hard, awful ones, but most of the people were grateful I'd made the call. And after that there was an amazing sense of relief and lightness. Nowadays I keep a rolling list where I'm always mopping up my own spills as I go along.

Plus, I always try and monitor the quality of the energy I'm giving out.

Mental energy

Mental energy - our thinking 'muscle' - is precious and should be used wisely. And it actually is a muscle - or at least an organ. The brain uses an enormous amount of energy running the complicated system that is us. Just 2% of our physical mass is our brain but it uses 25% of our energy, even when we're asleep! The brain is an amazing tool but it has a lot to do. The demands we make of it in work mode - to comprehend, decide, perceive, communicate - are only part of everything else it has to do.

High achieving people manage their mental energy carefully. The key is focus, being able, for as long as necessary, to block distractions before they take hold. This is a key skill that we can all get better at. It's about being truly present, in the here and now. Neuroscientists have started doubting whether 'multitasking' is actually possible. My wife would say those scientists are probably men, but in my experience you can do several things at once badly but real work takes concentration. Some days I spend 12 hours farting around, achieving little, while others I get what's needed done in 40

CHECK YOUR LEVELS

'Energy' is a complex thing. There are actually four types of personal energy and with care you can ensure a steady and increasing flow of all of them.

1. *Drive (Spiritual energy):* Identify your sense of purpose in work. Ask yourself: does this contribute anything beyond a salary for me and profit for my company?
2. *Quality (Emotional energy):* Are you taking responsibility for your own happiness and messes? Identify and clear up the resentment and rancour you've played a part in creating.
3. *Focus (Mental energy):* Write down the three results you have to achieve this week, focus on them and review your progress each day.
4. *Quantity (Physical energy):* Give yourself a break! Exercise three times this week, drink plenty of water and have a few early nights to catch up on your sleep.

Handy hint: Before you do something, whether it's chairing a five-hour meeting, making a phone call or writing a report, ask: Why do this? What's the point? Is it 'on purpose'? If yes, proceed and watch your energy rise and the difference you make. If the answer is no, challenge the need to do it.

Further reading: Check out *On Form*, by Jim Loehr and Tony Schwartz. Also check out the European Foundation for Quality Management (EFQM) business excellence model (www.efqm.org). Sounds dull, I know, but it really helps you measure the exciting and less tangible success factors in a business.

minutes. The trick is to identify the right commitment and focus your mental energy on it, like focusing sunlight through a magnifying glass. When I'm tired I can feel, almost physically, my mental hard drive fragmenting.

One way to focus is to cut big things down into bite-sized chunks. When I raced in the Ironman triathlon - 2.5 mile sea swim followed by 112 miles on a bike and then a marathon – I got round by focusing on nothing but the next lamppost.

Physical energy

This is our general fuel level. Without it we can't make good use of our spiritual (drive), emotional (quality) and mental (focus) energies. It's actually better than renewable. It's magic. (The more you use the more you get.)

Prepare now for common sense.

I work on my physical energy by:

- *Keeping fit:* Physical exercise is brilliant for reducing stress and rebooting your hard drive. The magic part is, the more you exercise, the fitter you get and the more fun exercise is. And the more energy you have. I do it for me, my family and my customers, all of whom deserve an energised version of me.

- *Eating well:* Every meal should include fresh fruit and vegetables and complex carbohydrates. A diet heavy on salty, greasy, sugary stodge will pile on the pounds, deprive you of vitamins and minerals and give you short energy peaks and long energy troughs. Fruit, veg and complex carbohydrates are better for your digestive system and release energy consistently over a longer period of time. Avoid too much coffee and tea and drink plenty of water.

- *Rest:* Getting a good night's sleep in a blacked out room is essential. Most of our learning and recuperation takes place in sleep: we recover, literally, from the day. I say a blacked out room because light inhibits the production of melatonin, the hormone that regulates sleep. So we're not maximising recovery if we sleep in a room awash with light pollution.

Also remember that sleep hormones are getting the better of us again between 1pm and 3pm, which is when most of the sensible world has a siesta! If you can't have 40 winks after lunch, try to use the time to open post and answer emails. Do the low-level stuff around this time and save the morning for focused mental work.

Rest also means unhooking regularly from work so you can return fresh. Use holidays and weekends. It's not shirking: your productivity depends on it.

10. The Evolving Leader
WHAT DO YOU NEED TO UNLEARN?

"The righter you do the wrong thing, the wronger you become.
If you make a mistake doing the wrong thing and correct it, you
become wronger." – Russell Ackoff

I want to talk about stupidity for a minute.

As an operations manager, up until I was about 40, I approached every project as if I was backed into a corner, battling it out with the client, the designers, subcontractors, even my own colleagues. And because that's the way I pictured it and behaved, that's pretty much the way it was.

I was successful, award-winning even, but it was hard work. Hard for the teams, hard for me and, because I was often stressed, hard for my family.

Now I'd like to think I'd approach things differently. For starters I'd trust people a lot more, give them the space to find solutions and work through issues themselves. I wouldn't see everything as a potential threat to my authority and hence to the progress of the job.

Was I stupid back then? I don't think so. I'd done a tough degree in civil engineering. In fact I was kind of a closet academic, in my spare time writing papers on technical and management issues for academic journals. I actually thought of myself as one smart cookie. And yet, when it came to my perceptions and to the way I behaved, I had this fairly sizable blind spot.

I've met some very narrow people, some very ignorant people, some highly inflexible people – but not many actually 'stupid' people. Apart from being a convenient label to slap on to people or things we don't like, 'stupidity' is not a very useful concept for understanding people.

But I want to talk about stupidity because a leader has got to be whatever the opposite of stupid is. And I don't just mean clever, savvy, intelligent, the way I thought I was. I mean wise.

There's a thing called the Knowledge Hierarchy. It has been developed and argued over by boffins for decades, but leaving the finer points aside, it's a great tool for thinking about what we know. Generally we start earning a living up around the Knowledge level, when we've got a handle on how to do something somebody will pay us for. But with leadership you've got to push upwards into Understanding and (gulp!) Wisdom.

The late Russell Ackoff, an American organisational theorist credited with articulating the Knowledge Hierarchy roughly as it appears here, once told an audience: "The righter you do the wrong thing, the wronger you become. If you make a mistake doing the wrong thing and correct it, you become wronger. If you make a mistake doing the right thing and correct it, you become righter. Therefore, it is better to do the right thing wrong than the wrong thing right."

It's the difference between *efficiency* and *effectiveness*.

So how do you get wisdom?

Experience is essential. I doubt if real wisdom is possible without it. But experience takes a long time to collect. And, in these fast-changing times, leaders often have to make a judgement on something they have no specific experience of. What then? Experience is good, but if we relied only on experience we'd be long dead before we'd stored up enough to deal with everything that might come our way.

Also, there actually may be a downside to experience.

In his book *What Got You Here Won't Get You There*, American coach Marshall Goldsmith makes the brilliant observation that in our fluid and fast-changing world all your hard-won understanding of how to do what you do might over time become counter-productive if you're dogmatic about its worth. We're the sum of our experiences, beliefs, environment, mentors and parents, bosses and education, but all that's in the past. These influences shape who we are but they may also limit our potential. Goldsmith's challenge to us is to stop and ask 'What do I have to *un*learn, here?' Do we have the humility to check these things out to see if they're still of value? Most people have zero curiosity about the workings of their inner selves. Your market is changing. Your organisation is changing. Your customers are changing. Are you changing?

One way of seeking wisdom is to put yourself on perpetual, personal blind spot patrol. Your intellect should always be getting stronger and more agile, capable of

The Knowledge Hierarchy

WISDOM
Future facing. 'What's
the right thing to do?'

UNDERSTANDING
'Why?' territory. Also, the capacity to
synthesise new knowledge from old

KNOWLEDGE
Information combined to be useful in
answering 'How?' type questions.

INFORMATION
Data combined to answer questions like *who, what, where* and *when*

DATA
Quantities and stuff, represented by symbols

identifying, understanding and using new perspectives. We see really talented people and teams in this business hobbled by narrowness. Like the project leader who can't engage with the design team because he's decided that all architects are up in the clouds. Or delivery teams focused so completely on their own processes that they can't fathom the urgent and shifting priorities of their clients.

How do you stay on personal blind spot patrol? It's a tall order. Get generally better informed, all the time, about everything, including yourself and how you work.

Reading is one way. Some people aren't big readers. Maybe you're not. Maybe you don't have the time, or you see it as a chore, or somehow the right books or articles just never come your way. That's understandable, but we're not going to let you off the hook. Reading is a key part of a balanced intellectual diet. Things go deep when you read, deeper than listening to a recording or watching a documentary. You're actively participating, making pictures in your head, questioning, testing, arguing back, rather than just passively receiving.

Talking to new people is great. I know a chairman of a company who makes a point

BLIND SPOT SEARCH AND DESTROY

Power tool n°10

1. Choose a conundrum, something that bugs you about the work you're doing, your industry or your company. It should be in the realm of Understanding, a 'Why?' question. If you're delivering school buildings it might be 'Why do teachers make such difficult clients?' (Just an example.)

2. On a sheet of paper write down a series of statements, what you consider to be the 'givens', as you see them, about the situation surrounding the conundrum.

3. Next write down a series of answers to the 'Why?' question. Don't worry about them being balanced or correct, just make sure you're recording what you feel is the truth.

4. Next write down a series of actions you'd take, if you had the power, to resolve the conundrum.

5. Now do one month of targeted horizon expansion on that conundrum. This should include:

   a. Read. Locate some current articles or blogs about school building programmes written by teachers or anyone with a perspective different to yours.

   b. Connect: Have three quality conversations with teachers or, again, any stakeholder whose perspective is foreign to you. Ask questions and listen carefully. If you find that hard, write "W.A.I.T." on the back of your hand. It stands for Why Am I Talking?

   c. Experience. Attend a public meeting of school trustees or of the local education authority to see what they're all about. Offer to swap a guided tour of your construction site for a guided visit to a school in action.

6. Go back to the sheet of paper and carefully read it. As necessary, rewrite and refine the Conundrum, the Givens, the Reasons and the Actions. Notice how your thinking about the conundrum has evolved. If no refining is necessary, you're a genius and we apologise for having wasted your time with this chapter.

of taking someone new out to lunch about once a month, and it has nothing to do with business schmoozing. He explained it to me: 'People are portals into other worlds. They help you make sense of your own.' I find that inspiring. Not all of us have the interpersonal gifts or the expense accounts to do what he does but we can all talk to people and be politely inquisitive and curious. It's the difference between treating every encounter as a chance to parade what we know and treating every encounter as a chance to increase what we know.

Visiting new environments is also great. Most professional institutes put on study tours and site visits, and they're often undersubscribed. Trying new things works, too.

The most evolved people we meet have a natural sense of wonder and curiosity about the world and about themselves. They're willing to look inwardly (without navel gazing) to see what makes them effective or ineffective. They're willing to interrogate themselves and to spot areas of understanding foreign to them. They find these areas *enticing*. In our forums, these people stand out. In a hectic, knowledge-based debate they floor everybody with a nugget of wisdom. They're often the people talking the least, and the least attached to their opinion.

Would you go to a heart surgeon or cancer specialist who was even a year behind in her own continuing professional development? Not likely. Why is it any different for leaders in business or any kind of service delivery? Getting down to brass tacks, leaders ought to broaden their minds for the following list of reasons, some of them shamelessly pragmatic.

Being curious about what makes people tick will help you understand and empathise with the different sorts of people in your team, which will help you connect with them better and get more out of them.

Being able to talk to a wide variety of people will continually refresh your understanding of your specific challenge.

Your judgements about your project or task will be better if you have a deepening understanding of how it sits in the broader context – the company, the sector, the industry, the economy, the country, the world.

People will trust and admire you more if you're broadly well informed and worldly wise. (But NOT if you're a show-off.)

An active, enquiring mind is more fun and makes you more attractive to the opposite sex.

Apparently there are two competing theories of intelligence out there. One, called 'incremental theory', holds that it doesn't matter how much intelligence you were born with because you can always get more. I like this one. It means we can always do perpetual horizon expansion. It means that with the right mindset I can be wiser, more effective and more interesting to talk to at 50 than I was at 40.

The other theory, called 'entity theory', says that no, you're born with your ration of intelligence and that's your lot. Whatever you try, you'll never get any smarter.

I don't like this theory.

I think it's stupid.

The information trap

In technical industries a high premium is placed on Information and Knowledge, and for good reason. But sometimes it gets in the way of Understanding and Wisdom. Here's an example.

We did a workshop once for a project that had hit the buffers. Communication had ceased and everybody was drafting their notices of claim. We applied our standard breakdown technique for the group but it was really hard going, with blame and accusations over this or that detail flying back and forth all morning. Then, at lunch, the 'principals', the client, the architect and the MD of the contractor, took themselves off for a private conflab. They were gone for a few hours and an amazing thing happened. Almost of its own accord the discussion moved up several levels, from widgets and who said what to whom, to strategies and shared visions. The atmosphere became electric. People who'd grimly sat all morning with their arms crossed suddenly sat up and were talking animatedly.

But then the 'principals' came back. They sat down sourly, rolled up their sleeves and said, 'Right. Now what about those widgets?' Several attempts were made to fill them in on what had happened but they insisted on diving straight back down into the detail. The energy in the room plummeted again. People were really hacked off.

11. The Failing Leader
WHERE DO YOU NEED TO BE FAILING?

Stress is us trying to keep our comfort zones intact while external forces do their damnedest to pull them apart.

Frazzled. Scared. That's what many of our clients are these days. "Stressed" doesn't do it justice. They're frazzled and scared.

"If we don't get some orders in the next couple of weeks we've got maybe four months before we're in real trouble," one client admitted recently.

We approach the topic of failure carefully because it's easy to sound glib about it. However, failure in general is necessary if people and teams are ever going to get better at what they do.

With frazzled and scared clients we try and explore this important fact: Stress is our brains resisting change. Stress is us trying to keep our comfort zones intact while external forces do their damnedest to pull them apart.

Our job as coaches is to challenge clients – whether they're fighting against stagnation or fighting for survival – to go further, to take chances at things they may not succeed in, to risk being vulnerable.

Leaders should be asking regularly: where do I need to be failing?

Let's break it down. We think there are three areas where leaders should be introducing the risk of failure: personal performance, team performance and ventures.

Personal performance

One of Paul's coaching clients – we'll call him John – earned respect in his company for being a sober, thoughtful guy who never spoke rashly or made decisions without careful consideration. When he spoke up in a meeting you could count on some piece of crystallised wisdom – a gem, in other words.

But when he became MD his style started getting on people's nerves. Him sitting there not saying much was being interpreted as reticence, as indecisiveness, as preferring to let others stick their necks out and look stupid, and even as vacuousness.

He knew he had to do some blurting. In the mêlée of decision-making around the boardroom table – the company was going through a scary time – he had to be in there with the rest of them. He had to lead, even if what he was leading was a muddle. He had to risk the unthinkable – saying something daft.

So he worked on that. He mucked in. And the results were dramatic. Before, boardroom "discussions" tended to bog down into unproductive stand-offs. Sensing no leadership from him, people hardened their positions and waited to see which side he would take. Now, by asking dumb questions, venturing off-the-cuff opinions and generally showing what he didn't know, people followed him down into the murk. The result was a more exploratory, less ego-driven environment that engendered confidence, engagement and a sense of common purpose.

If you want to build your leadership muscle, if you're really going for it, failure is part of the territory. In physiological terms you promote muscle growth and strength by tearing it by exertion. Skinned knees are a normal part of learning to ride a bike, and mouthfuls of seawater are a normal part of learning how to surf.

Team function

Leaders don't need to court failure here because teams are just prone to it. The trick is learning how teams can benefit from failure.

Partnership working is currently seen as one of the great ways forward, but 'partnership' suggests everybody should like each other. Clearly, this would be no bad thing but it's not realistic and tension is part of what makes relationships great.

There's a coaching term, 'breakdown', which describes this lapse into dysfunction. (I say 'lapse' but what I really mean is 'normal progress'.) Breakdown is good. It's an opportunity to call time on a situation, to look at what isn't working and why rather than shift blame around. To capitalise on breakdown, as coaches, we sometimes let arguments progress in group sessions to get issues, opinions, misconceptions, egos all on the table. That way they can be tackled, instead of danced around.

Debriefing is another key technique. Often, we're uncomfortable with it, usually because we've had bosses who invited honest feedback but when it came they tended to lash out defensively or shut the discussion down.

The idea of debriefing is to look at team failures to identify lessons, not scapegoats. Even small failures provide lessons. In mature relationships it's okay to have discussions about failure. If that's acknowledged, it can be dealt with. It's the avoidance that costs. Coaching works to deconstruct failures, so that leaders get to work through coaches to free themselves up for their next plan. Teams need time to heal the legacy issues and forgive each other. Forgiveness is a sign of strength - the weak never forgive.

Ventures

This could be launching a new business unit, entering a new market or developing a new service offering. It's where we're most risk-averse because we're asking the organisation to bet valuable resource on us and if it fails there's nowhere to hide.

It's easy for us to shout "That's it! Go on! Over the top!" from the sidelines, but leaders do need to push their organisations out of their comfort zones, or risk stagnation.

We do believe, though, that with ventures there's bad failure and good failure. Bad failure uses absolutely everything up: there's no money or credit left, your reputation is shot, nobody will trust you or even speak to you and your own confidence is destroyed. Good failure leaves a little something left in reserve so you can pick up the pieces, especially your own confidence, and carry on.

Ever heard of 'The Peter Principle'? Put forward by Dr. Laurence Johnston Peter in the late 60s, it was a slightly jokey theory that people get promoted upwards in an organisation until they reach their 'level of incompetence' - the job they can't really do very well - and there they stay, desperately trying not to rock the boat lest they be exposed.

It's an unkind image, but useful sometimes for waving in front of executives who are over-afraid of failure, or who can't distinguish between disaster and stepping out of a comfort zone.

Where should you be failing? Which leadership muscle do you need to tear or push? Is it standing by your viewpoint? Building your championship team? Taking a risk with a venture?

It used to be that 'Failure Is Not An Option'. Seems to us that for those wanting to push their limits and lead their people and business to greater success, failing is not only an option, it's required.

THE MANAGED SCREW-UP

Power tool n°11

1. Identify a thing your team can't do but should be doing.
2. Tell them you'd like the team to be able to do this and explain what the rewards are if they can do it.
3. Start team training for the capability, and explain what managed failure could look like.
4. Find a team elsewhere in the organisation or in another organisation and enlist them as training partners.
5. Warn people up and down the command chain, saying 'This may not work, but...'
6. Go on! Over the top!

12. The Fearful Leader

YOU THINK YOU'RE THE ONLY ONE HAVING SLEEPLESS NIGHTS?

I spotted my guy coming down the central staircase, but there was something odd about the way he moved. He was gripping the banister like he was scared of falling.

Ten years of coaching has revealed to us the No. 1 personal fear among executives in this business. Put a stethoscope to the skull of many successful, up-together people and you will hear a little voice. It's saying: *"You're not actually very good, are you? I mean, at root, you're a bit of a sham. Admit it. And you're going to be found out!"*

I know this fear well. I left school at 16 with no clue what to do and worried I'd end up down the coal mine. I stumbled into a job as a trainee civil engineer. I got qualified, got promoted, and went on to being a suit with a BMW. Up to the age of 40 I worried someone would find out I wasn't really that clever. Then around that time I found myself in a meeting with the founder of a national contractor. We got talking and he admitted that his biggest fear was the same as mine! I was sat there thinking this bloke was the bees knees. He'd started a major company from scratch. He'd created all this and he was as daft as me! At a stroke the grip of that fear was loosened and it had a dramatic effect. Up to then a lot of what I did was to protect myself. I was doing defensive stuff, making sure no one found out if something was my cock-up. That creates a lot of negative energy and stress.

Since then, in meetings with dozens of executives, I've found that it's an incredibly common fear. And there's an equally common fear that's a close companion to that one. Little voice again: "*Here you are, awake at three in the morning, worrying again. Nobody else does this, you know. You're the only one. Have you ever stopped to appreciate how basically weird you are?*"

No! Fear is good. If you're a soldier you're taught to see it as a friend. Without it you'd fall asleep on watch or neglect to maintain your equipment. In business, if you have no fear you're probably delusional. But make sure you're afraid of the right things. Fear of the wrong things – wasted fear – hobbles you and saps your energy. Fearing the right things on the other hand, and dealing with those fears constructively, makes you stronger.

Recently I realised the world was getting me down. I was addicted to the news. Environmental disasters, war, disease, economic decline, corruption, deepening geopolitical tension, social decay, general craziness - from where I was sitting it seemed we were all going to hell in a handcart. Then I twigged that media organisations have a professional obligation not just to report facts but to tell 'stories', to weave narratives that grip us. I'm not saying, exactly, that most of what you hear isn't true, only that the choice of what you hear and how it's presented is all decided by ratings-hungry producers and editors. I also read the book *Risk*, by Dan Gardener, which lays out how,

The fear... of success

A while ago I ran into a guy I knew, the MD of a construction consultancy. I asked him how he was doing and he said okay but for the last 10 years or so turnover had been stuck at £20 million. Would I help him kickstart a strategic growth plan? I said sure. So we got the main board together in a room and I just asked the question - where do you want to be in five years? For two hours I stood waiting with my marker poised over the white board while they argued. 'Well, we could do this but then we'd lose that, or we could do that but then this would happen,' etcetera. Finally, out of frustration, the MD stood up and said: "For heaven's sake, give me that pen!" and he wrote '£45m' on the board. Everybody grumbled - 'Easy for you to write that!' 'Yeah, we're the ones who'll have to do it!' and so on.

Three years later turnover was £90 million!

in the war over ratings, journalists sensationalise statistically rare and low probability events. I won't repeat his statistics but believe me it's illuminating. We're being encouraged to fear stuff that will likely never happen. (Here's a story you won't hear on the news: *'Flash! Incontrovertible evidence shows we're living in the safest and most prosperous time ever in modern history!'*)

Anyway I kicked my news habit. I stopped listening. Instead I started listening more to my customers, to their fears and opportunities, because, to my business, that's all that matters.

The flip side of Dan Gardener's argument is that we're being distracted from high probability risks that we really ought to be mitigating. Take terrorism. What are the chances of being killed by a terrorist attack? A drop in the bucket compared to the chances of being knocked over by a car. I don't know anyone who's been involved in or even witnessed a terrorist attack. I know four people who've been knocked over by cars.

We need to identify real risks, face up to them, and make a plan. We're talking about sensible risk mitigation, by the way, not risk elimination. Elimination is what politicians try and sell us. Since 9/11 the US has spent trillions trying to eliminate the risk of terrorism, and where has that got us?

I sometimes feel the drive to eliminate risk in health and safety has reached ridiculous proportions. Recently I went for a meeting with an MD at his headquarters. I was bang on time, so imagine my pique when the receptionist told me I had to watch a safety video before I could enter the building proper. Fuming, I sat and watched the video. It told me among other things about first aid facilities, fire exits and warned me to be on guard for slip and trip hazards. (This was a corporate office.)

"Thank you," the receptionist said. "I'll tell Mr. X you're here."

I waited, and then spotted my guy coming down the central staircase. There was something odd about the way he moved. He was gripping the banister like he was scared of falling. When he finally made it down we shook hands and he invited me up, but when we got to the stairs he turned and said:

"Can I ask you please to take a firm grip of the banister as we go up?" Then he gave me a look and whispered: "Health and safety."

Executives actually have a pretty good handle on the real business risks out there. We've kept a tally of executive fears throughout a decade of workshops and, unlike the personal, phantom ones – *I'm a sham! I'm not good enough!'* – these are pretty sound.

Here are the top three in their current ranking:

I fear I'm not getting how my clients' needs are changing in this volatile market, that I'm missing the point.

I'm worried about maintaining motivation in myself and my people. I'm not strategic

TEA WITH THE BOGEYMAN

1. Write a list of your biggest business fears. Do it fast, without intellectualising.
2. Alongside each, score out of 5 the *probability* of that thing happening.
3. Alongside each score out of 5 the *impact* if it does.
4. Multiply the two numbers together to give a risk rating for each fear.
5. Underline the significant ones inside your sphere of influence and take action.
6. 'Elevate' the ones that are outside your sphere of influence. That means start talking about them with your boss and with trusted customers, even with peers outside your company.
7. Repeat for your best opportunities.
8. Communicate your thoughts to your team and get them to do the same.

enough – I keep going 'operational'.

Yup, these are good fears. But don't get seized up by them. Get to know them. Bring them into the room and sit them down. They're not that bad.

How are you with your fears? Forging ahead with a plan or stuck with your head in the sand? If you're full of fear you are sure to be transferring it to your people.

13. The Focused Leader

ARE WE REALLY BUSIER NOW THAN WE WERE BEFORE BLACKBERRYS?

Email creates a false sense of entitlement to each other's attention.

I don't want to be alarmist or anything, but distraction is a disease that's reaching epidemic proportions.

I really suffer from it. Every time an email comes in I stop what I'm doing and reply to it. Good job I don't get that many compared to our customers. I might get 10 or 15 a day. Some tell us they get 200.

It's a full-time job sitting there answering other people's stuff and waiting for replies to your stuff.

Paul recommends switching off your email alert and checking emails only twice a day. For savvy people face-to-face is the gold standard for communication. Compared to face-to-face, email is like old-fashioned post, and most of my post is junk.

Ignore lots of emails, too. Email creates a totally false sense of entitlement to each other's attention. Often what we're really saying with an email is: "This is what I'm thinking about. Can you think about it too? Right now?" Reading and responding to an email takes effort. Is that effort well spent and in line with your core accountabilities? If somebody really needs your attention they can come and see you.

My own coach tells me I should get rid of my physical office. I get the logic. In a project team or a business where does the really important stuff get done? Where is the money made? The problem solved? The customer won? The idea generated?

Is it sitting at your desk playing email polo?

In the last three years we've noticed in our workshops that whenever there's a break, people dive into their mobiles or PDAs. They used to talk to each other. Now they just sit there, tapping away with their styluses or giving their thumbs a workout. Some even do it during the sessions.

These workshops are about crucial stuff: building the team, integrating a joint venture, or even dealing with a project breakdown. They're about deepening connections and relationships.

Are we really busier or more laden than we were before BlackBerrys and PDAs came along? Can't whatever detail or decision or chat possibly wait until after we've got together to do this essential thing? Or is diving into electronic busy-ness just easier somehow than really engaging with people?

THE CODE OF EXECUTIVE FOCUS

1. Don't agree to a meeting unless it is essential to your core accountabilities.
2. Schedule downtime in your diary. Go into focus mode when you need to compose a thought, develop an idea, connect with somebody, read reflectively. No email, BlackBerrys, meetings or interruptions.
3. Open emails twice a day, at 10am and 4pm, for instance. Best is when you need a break or when your powers of concentration are lower, like after lunch.
4. Just call time on distractions: no phones or laptops in meetings, just unadulterated attention to the critical conversations.
5. Sit down with your PA and work out how they can cut out the distractions that come your way by 50%.
6. Build your concentration muscle by practising an activity that requires concentration, and feel the burn! (It's pretty difficult to multi-task when you're open water swimming, for instance.)

We noticed all this crucial attention draining off into the webosphere so three months ago we started asking people to hand in their gadgets at the start of workshops. We thought we'd get resistance but they love it - a day of complete freedom from distractions, and they achieve some great results when they're really 'present'.

Concentration is crucial to progress and learning, and we're in danger of losing the ability to concentrate. The blizzard of information, digital noise and distractions of the 24-hour workplace are overwhelming us.

We need a 'distraction management strategy'!

The medium is the message, said philosopher Marshall McLuhan. I didn't really get that until I saw how email, texts and PDAs were fracturing our attention. So often the point of a BlackBerry is not the message it carries, but the BlackBerry itself and the pointless busy-ness it engenders.

Nobel Prize-winning economist Herbert Simon put it brilliantly when he said that a wealth of information creates a poverty of attention.

Our attention is a finite resource. You can only give your attention to so many things. The more we're distracted the more difficult it becomes to tell where our attention should go. It's a serious issue because life is becoming more complex. In many projects, especially public-private ones, the web of stakeholder relationships is bewildering.

The more complex the world, the more we need to draw on the skills required to make sense of it: reasoning, reflection, patience, learning, problem solving and connection with the right people. How can you do that without paying attention?

How distractible are you?

Quality in work and thought requires focus, but many modern habits erode our ability to give 100% attention. Use this tool to rate how impervious to distraction you are. Be tough! Maximum marks of 100 is a lifetime achievement. Also jot down a consequence of a given habit, and some corrective action you can take.

Scoring: 1 = Yup, that's me!   10 = Nope, not me at all!

Habit	Consequence	Corrective action
My digital gadgets are always on, grabbing my attention		
I respond to interruptions instantly		
I am always in busy mode, just having to be doing something		
I schedule no time for reflection, deep thought or recovery		
I multi task		
I attend meetings that waste my time		
I travel to deliver messages when technology could do the job		
I have no strategy or mechanism for switching off from work		
I try to handle everything (versus letting some stuff go)		
I let other people inappropriately determine where my attention goes		
Total score out of 100		

14. The Happy Leader

At the first whiff of low morale HR lays on the big staff survey. All my experience suggests they're a waste of time.

J oin me for a minute as a fly on the wall at breakfast nooks, pub tables, site cabins, boardrooms, whatever, all across the land.

"What's the matter?"

"Nothing."

"Are you happy?"

"Not really."

"Why not?"

"I don't know."

"Are you unhappy?"

"Well, no."

"Are you sad?"

"No. I'm just sort of… fed up."

"Fed up with what?"

"Work. Stuff. You know."

"No I don't. What?"

"I'm just, well... bored."

Bingo! Did you catch it? The riddle of the ages solved - the opposite of happiness, or what we usually mean by 'happiness', is not sadness, but *boredom*. And what is the antidote to boredom? Excitement!

I wish companies would get this. They worry so much about whether their people are 'happy'. At the first whiff of low morale HR lays on the big staff survey. All my experience with staff surveys suggests they're a waste of time. First off, they ask questions that management want answers to and not the ones burning up the staff. And if management do happen to stumble on what's hacking people off it's they who decide what to do about it. Even then they rarely follow through, which makes it all worse than before.

Second, the staff survey ignores this fundamental truth: *Knowing what makes you unhappy doesn't make you happy.*

Anyway, ask people what would make them happy and some shoot back: 'More money!' But we know about money, don't we? Or a better car. Back in the days of company cars I broke the mould by getting a Ford Escort at the age of 26. It was the bees knees. For a whole week. Then I stopped at a junction and a bloke pulled up in a Ford Sierra. I thought, Wow! Get that and you've arrived. Within 18 months I had a Ford Sierra. The magic lasted a whole fortnight, after which it reverted to being just a car.

In his book *Drive: The Surprising Truth About What Motivates Us*, Daniel Pink exposes the shortcomings of 'scientific management', the theory that because work is boring and because people are lazy you have to reward compliance with pay and punish non-compliance with the sack. This theory, put out by the engineer Frederick Winslow Taylor in the early 1900s, was called 'scientific' because it harnessed people's rational drive to put food on the table. Pink says it doesn't work anymore. It was okay in the industrial age when most jobs were routine but now, when success in business requires passion and innovation, people need something more than money to give it their all.

In fact, as Pink shows from many studies, money is actually a rubbish incentive for the most important things we need from employees - creativity, problem-solving, inventiveness and conceptual thinking. Artists produce inferior work when commissioned. Asked to solve puzzles, people get stupider if you introduce cash rewards. One classic study took three groups of children, all of whom liked drawing in their spare time. Group 1 was shown a fancy certificate and told they'd all get one if they spent the session drawing. Group 2 were given their certificate as a surprise for drawing. And Group 3 - unlucky - just drew without expecting a certificate or being surprised with one. Two weeks later researchers secretly observed the children in their spare time and while children from groups 2 and 3 were drawing away like billy-o, the kids from Group 1 drifted off to do other things. Their conclusion? The expectation of a reward snuffed out their enjoyment of drawing!

Overall, he says, 'extrinsic' motivation - the promise of money or perks - often promotes short-term thinking, ruins the enjoyment of the activity, encourages short cuts and cheating, crushes creativity and diminishes performance. Think back to your own experience. Have you ever seen the scramble for quarterly turnover cut your company off from longer-term revenue streams?

So what do we need to do? Make more room for 'intrinsic' motivation. Unleash, as he calls it, Type I behaviour, 'I' for 'intrinsic', where people are free to accomplish great things for the sake of it. Because they're *engaged*.

Because they're *excited*.

Because they're happy.

Pink's recipe for encouraging Type I behaviour has three ingredients:

Mastery: Give people the opportunity to get better at something they care about, not for money or brownie points but out of the joy of getting better at something they care about.

Autonomy: Give people control over how they do what they're supposed to do, including the hours they do it in and the people they do it with.

Purpose: Give people a sense that what they're doing has a purpose beyond just them drawing a salary and lining the pockets of shareholders. (For more on this see "The Inspired Leader".)

Sounds pretty far-fetched, right? Well, Pink found companies who actually do it. Like the software company that instituted a results-only-work-environment (ROWE), where nine-to-five went out the door and employees come in whenever they want, for as long as they want, as long as they get the job done. Or the do-anything-you-want idea, where employees use a percentage of company time (15% to 20%, for instance) to work on a project of their own choosing - the intellectual property staying with the company, of course. Under schemes like this, working all night and cackling away in their cubicles, happy staff produced the Post-It note for 3M, and Google Mail for Google.

Again, to us this may seem like a mildly interesting form of life in a galaxy far, far away, but Pink insists that harnessing Type I behaviour is the way of the future. Not only does it send a jolt of excitement throughout firms, it also produces results nobody could have predicted. His crowning example of the relative power of 'intrinsic' and 'extrinsic' motivation is the story of Microsoft's MSN *Encarta*, the bold undertaking launched in 1993 to create the world's first digital encyclopaedia. Expert writers and editors were paid to craft articles on everything under the sun. Microsoft's finest managers were tasked with launching it as a CD-Rom and later as a website. Business development people built up revenue streams in online subscriptions, CD-Rom sales and online advertising. It spent millions buying up *Funk & Wagnalls* and *Collier's* encyclopedias. But despite throwing everything it had at the project, Microsoft had to pull the plug on December 31st 2009, admitting that people just didn't look up information that way anymore.

Now, says Pink, compare that to Wikipedia. Launched in 2001 by a handful of enthusiasts, Wikipedia by 2009 had become the seventh most visited website in the world, its 16 million articles in more than 240 languages contributed and edited by volunteers, for the hell of it, because it made them happy.

There will always be a place for 'extrinsic' motivation - used carefully! - but good leaders will find ways of setting their people free, allowing more autonomy, mastery and purpose in work. I believe construction is naturally suited to that anyway, but our default setting is still the old Type X ('X' for 'extrinsic') - carrot-and-stick, command-and-control, bark, bollock and bite. But, you say, what would autonomy, mastery and purpose look like for us? We've got some tips for you (see below) but the real answer will come in different forms depending on you and your teams.

And what about you? Are you excited? People think excitement is for the lucky few but I believe excitement is something you can pursue, whatever you're doing. Excitement acts on people like energy acts on atoms - it makes them start jumping around. When I'm excited, I'm really happy, my energy is great and so are my results, so I make an effort to inject thrill into my life, whether it's work or not. How? For me, creating things is exciting, and that could be new business opportunities, real customer value or environments for people to succeed in. Learning new things is exciting. New challenges are exciting. Doing scary things is exciting. I still take an annual ski holiday even though I've been injured every single time I've gone. Leading a workshop with 100 people can also be scary, especially when 99 of them resent being there at first.

And are you *exciting*? Do you channel and amplify energy or do you lure it into a dark alley and strangle it? Are you tuned in to what excites your people and your customers or do you expect them to crawl into your nook or cranny? I remember once going for an interview for a framework partnership with a big client. We spent 15 minutes droning on about our record on time, budget and quality before the client asked us to stop. "If I didn't think you could deliver that, you wouldn't be here talking to me," she said. "As you know we're constantly in the public eye, so we were kind of hoping to hear what you guys do for the community, the environment, that sort of thing?" What a great lesson! We'd effectively bored ourselves out of a job!

So the next time you see a long face, whether on an employee, a customer, a loved one or in the mirror, don't ask 'What would make you happy?' because people rarely know the answer to that. Instead ask 'What would make you excited?' They'll tell you, if you're prepared to listen.

THE THRILL INJECTION

1. *Do an excitement audit:* Ask 10 of your people what would really excite them about the project they're on, about the direction of the business, about their careers. Be patient – they may think it's a trap. And if you butt in you'll lose it. Look at the responses and be alert to great ideas for the business, and for practical ways you can release Type I behaviour in the short, medium and long term. You'll find this much cheaper and way more useful than a staff survey.
2. *Do whatever you want (for beginners):* Can we do the Google and 3M thing of letting people work on whatever they want for some of the time? I don't know. But how about this adaptation: Once a month take an operational issue, or a strategic challenge (like landing a new customer or entering a new market) and let people organise themselves into task teams to solve it. Even people who wouldn't normally get involved at that level. (Warning: no cash prizes!)

Further reading: Check out *The 4-Hour Workweek*, by Tim Ferriss. I'm indebted to him for the great insight on excitement vs. boredom. And, of course, Daniel Pink's *Drive: The Surprising Truth About What Motivates Us* – but only if you're prepared to have your mind opened.

15. The Important Leader

HOW DO YOU FIT INTO THE GRAND SCHEME OF THINGS?

The average effectiveness of teams is only 28%. So... um... yeah.
You're important.

My wife is a special needs teacher helping 6-to-10 year olds get a good start in life. Her sister is a nurse in a children's intensive care unit. In the Grand Scheme of Things, these are important jobs.

Then there's me and Paul. We help build team effectiveness in the construction industry.

Hmmm...

Teams were bumbling along before we turned up and will be long after we're dust. Would anyone really notice if Paul or I didn't turn up for the next month? Is what we do *important*?

It used to bother me, until I saw that I was approaching the question with an old and self-defeating kind of view of the industry, one that reduced it to merely: 'the tricky game of making money out of building'.

Viewed through this jaundiced prism, I'm not important. Nobody is, including clients and users.

But while construction is partly this, it's far more, too. If you lead a business unit, a project team or a company in the built environment business, you *are* important, and here are three reasons (among many) why.

1. You're on the front line in making the built environment happen.

This is what you do – forget for a moment about the commercial terms under which you do it. You make the buildings and structures that facilitate human life. It's the physical fabric of society. I don't think I'm being too philosophical here: we forget this.

I was involved in a job for a housing association once, a major refurbishment programme, and the project team agreed to a meeting with a representative of the tenants' association. She was 75 years old. She spoke passionately for the time allotted, about five minutes, offering great ideas, passing on important information and making some requests. She didn't complain. On the contrary she was full of gratitude – we were improving their homes, after all. It was clear she'd done a lot of groundwork for this one meeting, consulting widely and preparing notes. It crossed our minds that nobody was working harder on this project than she was, and she wasn't getting paid. We were humbled.

You may be building a school in a deprived area or a hospice for cancer patients, but you may also be building a trunk road or refurbishing a department store. That's okay. (I once led a three-million-pound new-build project for Rothmans, the cigarette company.) Our physical environment has a profound effect on us. Whatever it is, shabbiness, waste and error matter. Bad quality eats into society and drags us down whether we realise it or not. This goes not only for the thing that gets built, but the way in which it gets built. When I started out nobody gave a stuff about newts or archaeological remains or noise or dust and consequently when we built we used to make lives miserable, or at least difficult, for a lot of people.

2. You have a major but intangible effect on society.

Quality, transparency, efficiency, competitiveness, value-for-money, doing a great job for a fair price – these are fragile values that make this country one of the most desirable places to live in the world. These values may be propped up by laws but really they have life and impact because individuals – you and me – live by them, and societies that don't have them are poisoned with corruption, irresponsibility, falling standards, criminality, stagnation and decay.

3. You matter to your people.

There is a dark side to this industry and we've all seen it. The hours are long and the culture is adversarial. The effects include burn-out, family dysfunction and mental and physical health problems. Take one example: in the cut and thrust of a typical project where a mishap threatens to cost time and money (as they invariably do) individuals face off with daggers drawn. Traditionally there's been a fair bit of bravado around this but I've been in the thick of it and what never gets talked about is the personal toll it takes on the people involved.

It doesn't have to be this way. Effective leaders create work environments marked by pride, satisfaction and personal growth, ones that inspire, challenge and reward. At the other end of the spectrum, bad leaders create work environments filled with stress, confusion, conflict, fear, dissatisfaction and exhaustion. The former produces results and the team players come back for more. The latter produces failure and the exodus of talent.

So I have no doubt what you do is important, and I think what we do is important, too. Over the years we've developed a comprehensive diagnostic tool for teams to measure their own effectiveness and, since 2004, the average score teams have *given themselves* is 28%.

Think of that: 28% effective! It's hard to imagine how a team can do all it could be doing - for shareholders, clients, society and the team players themselves - with a 72% effectiveness gap. And I believe this gap has been papered over by 10 years of boom - companies expanded turnover in the 'spend, spend, spend' economy and profit was okay, except for the odd blow-out job. So no one really paid much attention

to team effectiveness, they just got on with it. Wind forward to 2010. The pressure is on to squeeze every last ounce of efficiency out of overhead and cost. Scythes are being sharpened all over the land. The danger is that organisations will cut without having really understood the value they could have been getting out of their teams in the first place.

We build teams, you lead them. Our work, yours and ours, is really important. We should embrace our importance. If we don't think we, or what we do, are important we'll treat ourselves, our work and our people as unimportant, and our lives and the lives of others will be devalued in real terms as a result.

BIG UP! `Power tool n° 15`

1. If you're feeling down about what you're doing, you may have fallen into a narrow and jaundiced view of how you fit into the grander scheme of things. You may need 'bigging up'. We recommend:
2. Get out and talk to your customers. Find out what their world is like and how what you're doing helps them reach their goals. If it's a building you're creating, there's no better inspiration than talking to the people who will be its actual end users.
3. Get to know the people in your team better. Get a sense of how this project or venture fits into their life goals and what they want to achieve through it. You'll get a genuine lift from creating an environment for your people to progress in.
4. Before you take an axe to overheads (i.e. headcount), stop and think. Are you cutting actual dead wood or just unrealised value?
5. Assemble your team and ask them what's getting in the way of their effectiveness.
6. Listen carefully - absolutely no response from you.
7. Have them self-assess their effectiveness as a team (we can provide you with the diagnostic).
8. Work out your plan together and implement it.
9. Watch out for magic and celebrate it.

16. The Inspired Leader
PSST! WHERE YOU'RE GOING - IS IT GOOD?

Good things don't happen unless we think them up.

One of our associates was seconded to a major contractor in 2001 and he was humbled, amazed even, to find such a gifted bunch of people - officer material, all of them. A while previously there'd been a lavish recruitment drive. He'd been in the industry a long time and could spot talent from a thousand yards. Sadly, though, they had no direction. They were running all over the place, chasing any old job and losing money hand over fist. It was like a beautiful racing yacht with the most experienced crew ever assembled. But they'd left the helmsman on shore, and they were just going round and round in big, pretty circles.

The executives we coach really worry about the way they put off 'strategy' and get mired in 'tactics', the day-to-day operational stuff. They're right to worry. Probably the most important thing for a leader is 'the vision thing'. You've got to:

1. Know where you are,
2. Define where you want to be, and
3. Inspire your people to get from one to the other.

Have you ever seen how a vision can shape the future? We have. When Paul started out he worked in the health and safety department of a major contractor whose safety record was terrible. Inspectors openly called them a bunch of cowboys. Then a new director came on board and he stood up and said, 'in two years we're going to win the industry's top safety award'.

Everybody thought he was crazy. But he knew it would happen and acted like he knew it would happen and soon everybody else was acting like that, too. Paul, a mere whippersnapper, found himself telling flinty old foremen they couldn't do what they'd been doing for 40 years anymore. They thought it was funny at first, but Paul had the confidence not to cave in because he knew his director was in the boardroom fighting his corner, with a chair-leg, a broken Evian bottle, whatever. Two years later they won the award.

We've seen whole companies transformed. A few of us were around when Sir Christopher Wates decided to spend millions dragging his stuffy, hierarchical – and failing – family firm into the 20th Century. It was a long and difficult process, but Wates is now one of the most successful and innovative of the majors.

Lives changed. Our associate Phil was there. He'd always thought he was required to 'bark, bollock and bite'. So, being a talented guy, he made himself as hard as nails. But when the enlightenment dawned he was exposed to better styles of management. "It was like the lights coming on," he says. "I realised I wasn't a 'bark, bollock and bite' sort of manager at all." So he stopped doing that and started enjoying work and getting better results.

I'm now going to say something that's a total cliché but also totally true: our thoughts create tomorrow. They do. Things don't happen unless we think them up. If we don't think them up, somebody else will think something up for us.

People talk about inspiration as if it's a random bolt of lightning you either get or don't. Real inspiration isn't like that. It can start that way, but not always. Real inspiration is a bit of a slog, actually. It might start with being thunderstruck with an idea while rodding the drains, and then the real work starts. It's an act of painstaking creation, like building scenery for model railways. The vision you build is where you're going, and a useful one will have certain characteristics:

1. It has to be good, a place you'd all really like to be.
2. It has to be achievable, but only just.
3. It needs detail. 'We're going to be the best!' is meaningless. If it's meaningless people feel invigorated for an afternoon and then revert to type. It might be slightly out of focus, but you should see definite shapes.

A word of warning: with 'the vision thing', bigger is not always better. It's easy to fall into the BHAG trap. (Big, Hairy, Audacious Goals.) There are plenty of inspiration peddlers out there with more charisma than sense who can work up a frenzy of unrealistic expectations. 'You can do anything! Your thoughts create tomorrow!' Yeah,

true, but...

We see a lot of BHAG madness. The catalyst is usually a terrible year. Shareholders peer down through the jagged profit-hole in the floorboards and start pounding the table, demanding drastic action. In a cornered and desperate organisation a kind of mass delusion can take root, stoked by people who either are deluded themselves or are willing to gamble with people's faith for their own ends. We've seen companies trading at a £19-million loss one year set out to make a £10-million profit the next, just by doing everything harder and faster. The result is always disappointment, followed by cynicism, because people feel silly at having been led a merry dance.

Some of us remember a formula put out by The Halifax back when it was a good old-fashioned building society. It said there are four things you need to build a company, and here they are, in order:

1. The right people doing the right things.
2. The right systems and processes.
3. The right customers.
4. Profit.

Note that profit comes last. The reason is, if you focus on profit first you foul the other things up. There's always stuff you can do to increase the bottom line - chase claims more aggressively, bid for every job under the sun - but without a fundamentally better business, any gains go 'flash' and then 'poof'.

Don't bother too much with numbers, either - revenue targets, margins, etcetera. People aren't generally inspired by numbers. They're oppressed and freaked out by them, but not inspired. Look at what the whole 'targets' thing did to hospital performance. If you want to do numbers, look at the really interesting numbers, like the percentage of new customers who stay with you, the percentage of talented staff who stay with you, or the turnover generated by new or improved services.

What really inspires people is meaning. What does this project or this company *mean*? For me? For us? Where are we going? That's a vision thing. Tired people see just another bunch of the usual pressures. An inspirational leader sees beyond those. They've got a clear picture in their heads. They say, Wait! I'll tell you what this project is *actually* about! This is where we're going!

This vision doesn't have to be 'worthy'. If you're building a primary school in a deprived area you can say 'we're going to give these poor kids a great new school', but you can't rely on altruism in this industry. What if it's an office refurb for British American Tobacco? Or just another speculative commercial development? What's so inspiring about that, in the grand scheme of things?

The meaning you think up should be more about your team's destiny. Most people want to grow. They want greater individual mastery, more autonomy, responsibility and recognition. They want glory (i.e. cool things to say on their CVs). They also want their companies to grow, in health and reputation. They want to be part of something successful. (All this is way more inspiring than the numbers, by the way.)

The skill here is to think up good meaning: relevant, bold, achievable. Simple but amazing for your team. It might be 'in five years we'll have so many happy customers we're not bidding on price anymore', or 'our supply chain works so well we just don't do claims', or 'we're going to break into that new market'. 'We're going to break even' will hardly do it for your people.

Now, you. Are you inspired? If you're not, you can't inspire. You can't give what you haven't got. First, you've got to come up with your vision. You can copy somebody else's, by the way. Just make it yours, and your team's. Spend time filling in the detail: the people you'll be working with, the things you'll be doing, what customers and the market will be saying about you. Get gripped by it. Then you have to hold it in your mind while you're down in the trenches, because nobody will see it as clearly as you, and you're going to need more enthusiasm than anyone else.

How do you get that? For me inspiration is that thrilling glimpse of something

INSPIRATE!

1. Write down a list of things that give you a lift and raise your spirits.
2. Heighten your awareness of them. For a week add to the list as you go about your business. Notice what inspires you and write it down.
3. At the end of the week review the list and plan how to get more inspiration next week.
4. Repeat till being inspired becomes a habit.

Further reading: *Made to Stick: Why Some Ideas Survive and Others Die*, by Chip and Dan Heath.

beautiful and rare. Being lifted out of the ordinary. Like confidence and energy, inspiration is something you can cultivate and protect. I get my inspiration from reading great books, talking to great people, cycling hard in the hills, listening to Radiohead, watching the autumn colours, watching my family grow, helping and seeing people achieve, connecting with people. I'm also inspired by getting feedback which suggests I am on the right track and learning new skills. This stuff gets me buzzing!

And how do you inspire? This is tricky. Good people around you take time to make their minds up. They'll watch to see if you really believe, if you're serious, if they can trust you to follow through. There's a lot at stake for them, remember – you're asking them to leave their comfort zones. They'll note whether your actions and words match up. They'll tune in to all the messages you broadcast, attitudes, body language, behaviour.

This is where many people falter. They can think it in their heads but it doesn't always come out. To be inspirational, you have to be a bit evangelical. There's got to be an emotional charge in your signal. It makes people sit up and listen. In our culture it's bad form to be fervent about anything except sport. Get over it! Your people need a sense that you have a plan. They need some of your inspiration. What we say to clients who need to make something big happen is: Who are you going to *be* in that room? What would *unstoppable* look like?

Also, you need to use the right language. Avoid writing vague mission statements. We see many vision, mission and change statements and most are awful. When Paul and I have teams talk about their vision of success there's lots of passion in the room but when they come to write it down it gets lost in the tortured words.

In their fantastic book, *Made To Stick*, Chip and Dan Heath point out that when CEO's take to the podium they have 30 years immersion in the logic and conventions of business, and the language just doesn't connect. When John F. Kennedy asked Congress for an extra $1.7 billion dollars for his space programme he really connected: "I believe that this nation should commit itself to achieving the goal, before this decade is out, of landing a man on the Moon and returning him safely to Earth," he said.

Brilliantly clear! Smart man. Had Kennedy been a CEO, the Heaths write, he'd probably have said: "Our mission is to become the international leader in the space industry through maximum team-centred innovation and strategically targeted aerospace initiatives," or some such gobbledygook.

For it to stick, the Heaths insist, the message has to be "Simple, Unexpected, Concrete and Credible".

Is yours?

17. The Irresistible Leader

PEOPLE LIKE TO FEEL EXCITED AND INSPIRED. ARE YOU LETTING THEM?

I used to try to get people on board by defining what was in it for them and presenting beautifully reasoned arguments. Then I'd get totally hacked off when they gave lip service but no real commitment.

Ever seen this? The MD decides to launch a big change programme. He has a website built, prints fancy brochures and explains his sparkling vision in a series of road-shows with bunting, fireworks, dancing girls and motivational speakers who used to be good at sport. He exhorts everyone to get on board, saying there's glory if we do and disaster if we don't. The result is usually the same: attentive faces, nodding heads, and silence. "Any questions?" he asks. "No? Okay. Let's do it!"

Six months later he's back, in a rage, demanding to know why nothing has happened yet.

I've always been fascinated by how you get commitment to a cause. We're back to emotions, by the way. Commitment, remember, is an emotion.

I used to be an engineer. Engineering is all about detail and when I first got promoted I thought my job was to dive into the detail. Then I worked out that to deliver difficult projects my job was actually to get people on board. But how? Approaching it logically, I tried working out what was in it for them and presented beautifully reasoned arguments. Then I would get totally hacked off when they gave lip service but no real commitment.

Were they stupid, or was it me?

This baffled me for a long time, until I read a book called *Brain Rules* by John Medina, who observed that we process things in a certain order.

1. Emotions first.
2. Then meaning.
3. Then details.

Why emotions first? Medina says it's all about the evolution of the brain. We've been on the planet for millions of years but for the vast majority of that time we were out on the savannah, engaged in a constant struggle for survival. If you think of the evolution of the brain as a 200-page book, he says, the first 199 and a half pages would be us as hunter-gatherers, dealing daily with starvation, exposure, lions and hostile tribes. A couple of paragraphs would be the dawn of agriculture, and modern, literate, city-dwellers would take up a couple of sentences at the end.

So, if you plopped Mr. Caveman down in Leicester Square he'd have pretty much the same brain as us.

The point is, we think we're all very civilised and logical but the fact is we're hair-trigger fight-or-flight machines.

People experience strong emotions when they're faced with change: excitement, maybe, for some, but fear and anxiety for many. As humans we resist change – even change that's good for us, like stopping smoking or switching off from work on those first few days of a holiday. It's one of our survival mechanisms and links back to preserving 'what works' in the quest for food, shelter and security.

The irresistible leader has to recognise that and not take resistance to change personally. Nor should we take it as a sign that it's time to up the ante and get tough – that only makes people dig in. Emotions, especially negative ones, have lives of their own. If they're expressed and recognised they release their grip. If they're quashed they fester and grow.

So to get real commitment you're going to have to welcome these emotions into the room. Let people talk. Encourage them. Echo back to them the words they use. If the new direction you want to take is half-sensible people generally talk themselves into it. If you argue, even nicely, you're quashing their emotions. If you say "Don't worry! I've got it all figured out!" and try to explain logically why their fears are unjustified, you're quashing their emotions.

You may win the argument, in which case people may go along with you intellectually for a while. But they won't commit.

You'll have minds but not hearts.

Sure, people ask 'What's in it for me?' but what they usually mean is "What does this *mean* for me?" Plus, they're usually less selfish and demanding than we think. People like to get excited and inspired. They want to buy in. And people with their hearts in something will do whatever it takes to get the job done.

Sorry, we don't do emotions

We were asked once to help launch a change programme at a major international firm. Talking it over with the head guy, we decided to start first with the main board of directors. He said he really needed commitment, buy-in, inspiration, etc.. No problem, we said. We're used to working at the emotional level.

"I'll stop you there," he said. "These guys are all middle-aged, grey-suited engineers. They don't do emotions."

We explained that commitment, buy-in and inspiration were nothing but emotions.

"Okay," he said, "just don't use that word, emotions."

So we didn't. The first part of the day was Power Point presentations. Then after lunch we went around the room asking them questions about the change programme. What are you concerned about? What's exciting for you? What are you confident about? What do you need? Simple stuff, and the energy in the room shot up dramatically. All this real stuff came pouring out. They couldn't stop talking. There were big issues to resolve, but they were definitely on board.

THE BIG CONVERSATION

 Power tool n° 17

1. When you've defined your big vision, engage your own emotions. Write down (don't think, just write) your concerns, what's exciting for you about it and what makes you feel confident. Remember, you need to be committed, too.
2. Get your people in a room. Set out your big vision.
3. Invite emotions in. Ask questions about positive and negative ones. What's exciting about this? What makes them feel confident about it? What gives them concern about it?
4. Listen. Don't discuss, correct or even try to reassure them, just listen.
5. Repeat these conversations privately with key individuals, and tell them your concerns, too.
6. Informed by what you hear, jointly decide how to proceed.

Further Handy Tip: Getting real questions after a presentation is like pulling teeth. The problem is, most people don't know what they think until they've actually said it. They can't ask a question because it's not formulated yet, or they're worried it will come out clumsily. To help things along, first get them to write down what they thought was interesting or important. Then get them to talk to the person sitting next to them about what they've written down. You'll see the energy in the room go up. After a couple of minutes ask if there are any questions. By then people have had a chance to externalise thoughts and you won't be able to shut them up.

18. The Reflective leader

LAST TIME YOU SHOT FROM THE HIP DID YOU HIT THE TARGET OR YOUR TOE?

Be responsible – response-able – able to respond the way you, and not your wild emotions, choose.

Have you had days like this?
It starts with…

- A late train
  … and unfolds disastrously until the tally includes:
- 75 unread emails
- A four-inch stack of unopened post and drawings
- An injury on site
- A complaint from a neighbour
- Unsolicited 'feedback' from a colleague (bad)
- A legal notice of claim
- An angry call from the client
- A dumb question from a subcontractor

- Notification of a lost tender
- Discovery of a big, costly mistake
- An urgent request from your boss at 7pm, just as you were leaving, finishing with
- A personal slight from a loved one.

Have you had days like this? I've had days like this. And how did I react to each of these choice little surprises? 'Cool as a cucumber,' I'd like to say. But you know and I know that would be a big porky pie.

Stuff from the world hits us all the time. However fast we respond, there is a gap between the stuff hitting and our response to it. You might struggle to slide a sheet of rice paper into that gap, but it's there.

You need to mind that gap. Or I should say *don't* mind that gap. Love it, I mean. Make it longer. Wallow in it. Inside that gap are hidden treasures: answers to your burning questions, balms for your hurt and anger, little defusing kits for the bombs waiting to blow apart your networks and achievements.

I first cottoned on to this when I read Victor Frankl's book, *Man's Search for Meaning: The Classic Tribute to Hope from the Holocaust*. Even in the desperate environment of the concentration camps Frankl created a life for himself by refusing to give up control of his own mind. The only way remaining for him to do this was by choosing his own response to the insanely terrible things that were happening all around him. By reacting deliberately instead of instinctively he kept sovereignty over the last bit of himself remaining.

That really got me thinking. No matter what happens it's my response that counts. That's what ultimately defines me as a person and leader. And I can take control of my response. I can be response-*able*.

Watching the Isle of Man TT race on television, it struck me that motorbike racers have virtually no gap at all between the stimulus coming at them at 200 miles an hour - as they approach a corner - and their response. So to survive, let alone win, they have to be incredibly fit, mentally as well as physically. They're making instantaneous win-or-lose, life-or-death judgements. One of them was wired up to a heart-rate monitor and his ticker was going at 200 beats per minute around the course. No wonder, given that 231 people have been killed doing the race since it started in 1907.

Anyway, hats off. In construction it can sometimes feel like your heart's going 200 beats a minute, which is all the more reason to pause before you react.

I remember a piece of work I did with a construction team where the client wrote a two page letter to the contractor's project manager. He got it on a Friday, took offence and together with his commercial manager spent all that afternoon along with most of Saturday and Sunday compiling, fact-finding, editing and perfecting a six-page response with supporting appendices. They emailed it to the client on Monday, who was, in turn, gob-smacked. For the following six weeks, an increasing number of staff on both sides got involved in an all-out email broadside. Thousands of words were generated, and virtually no communication.

In one of our workshops with the team I asked what was upsetting them so much. It slowly emerged that the client had genuinely wanted to understand aspects of the project and so he wrote the letter. In the workshop, he explained that he sometimes didn't express himself clearly face to face – "sometimes it just comes out all wrong," he said – so he decided to write down his queries.

PAUSE FOR EFFECT-IVENESS

`Power tool n°18`

Now, next time you're sideswiped by something:

1. Breathe.
2. Re-holster your six-shooter.
3. Do something physical. Trot up some stairs, go for a brisk walk. Exercise siphons off adrenalin. Don't break things. Popping crisp packets is okay.
4. Calmly eat the crisps you've dumped on the desk.
5. Take a pen and paper and spend 10 to 30 minutes writing notes on your thoughts and feelings. Don't analyse, just write.
6. Read it through and reflect.
7. Decide what is important, with a bias toward 'the greater scheme of things'.
8. Decide how much time you really have to act or respond.
9. Let every minute of that period of time elapse before acting.

Further handy tip: The red-mist email
When you get an email that makes you see red and you can't help dropping everything to compose an indignant reply, do me this one small favour: remove the person's email address from the 'To:' field. Just leave that field blank. Then you can vent all you like without accidentally pressing the Send button before you're *really* ready to send.

Memorise this:

STIMULUS ⟶ GAP ⟵ RESPONSE

He went on to say that he was shocked and mystified at the response he got, and also by the ensuing war of words.

Opening up, the contactor's project manager said he was annoyed by the letter (it 'came out all wrong' in the end anyway) but that in hindsight he'd reacted badly. We decided to devote three hours of the workshop to the issues, and with all the heat and emotion dissipated it became clear that the upset was all about the upset and not the project or the contractor's performance. It was all something and nothing.

I used to be a hip-shooting, hot-headed operations manager. Now when something smacks into me from left field and gets my heart hammering I mind the gap, delaying my response when I can - and really, when *can't* you? - at least until I've slept on it or run it by someone else. If it isn't operationally urgent I'll let two or three days pass before I respond, and it's actually fun to watch my inner volcano cool and settle down, and to notice my thinking get strategic and more sophisticated.

And quite often in that widening gap the situation resolves itself. Just recently I had a red-mist email from a guy I'm collaborating with on something. I couldn't believe the line he was taking. It felt like he was wilfully forgetting several earlier conversations, was lying, and was bent on causing me huge inconvenience, all at the same time. Bewildered, disappointed and angry, I climbed right up onto my high horse and started composing an email in the most scathing and indignant tones I could muster. (Emails are great for that.) Then I stopped and went for a cycle. Then I had a meal and chatted with my wife. Then I did some other work. Then I watched a bit of TV, read a book and turned in. The next day I got on with some other things in the morning and some *other* other things in the afternoon. Then towards evening the phone rang. It was him. Having sort of forgotten about his idiotic email I was pleased - almost - to hear from him.

He hemmed and hawed for a bit, and then he said, "So did you get my email?"

"Yes I did," I said pleasantly. I was having fun now.

"Yeah, uh… The thing is…" he said, and went on, not to apologise exactly, but at least to ruefully explain the circumstances and why it had come out like that, and to ask me nicely for the favour he'd been stumbling ineptly towards in his stupid email.

And it was no problem to help him out.

Mind that gap! We think our response is so urgent. But it's almost always just the urgency of our feelings - the need to hit back, to lash out. Be responsible. Response-*able*.

Able to respond the way you, and not your wild emotions, choose. The alternative is being what Frankl refused to be - a victim, pushed around in your head by circumstance and other people.

If, like me, you shoot from the hip, lengthen the gap, give yourself time to think and reflect. If on the other hand you procrastinate for ages before reacting then maybe shorten the gap and go for progress rather than trying to reach perfection.

19. The Time Leader

WHY ARE YOU ACTING LIKE YOU'RE GOING TO LIVE FOREVER?

Imagine you could only work five hours a day. Break that rule and you and your family will be locked up.

'll be quick with this one!

In our workshops and executive coaching sessions the biggest issue by a mile is time. There's just not enough of this stuff to go around.

We said earlier in The Energetic Leader that time management is old hat, and that the focus should be energy management. That's true, but effective leaders must get to grips with time as well.

The first step is to stop kidding yourself that one day you will 'find' more of it, the way BP or Shell scour the globe for one more mother lode of easy oil. This fantasy will have you forever entangled and flailing. Time is a fixed commodity. Twenty-four hours a day is all you get. Accept this. Start living it, right now, before your most precious and utterly non-renewable resource is used up.

The next step is to understand once and for all that having enough time is only achieved by hard choices and great habits. You don't find time, you *make* it, and it's a difficult, often messy process.

I used to be terrible at time, when I was salaried and even more when I went into business for myself. Then about eight years ago I had a session with Dan Sullivan, the entrepreneurial coaching guru, and he told me about his concept of dividing your time into Focus days, Buffer days and Free days.

Focus days are when your nose is to the grindstone and you're totally focussed on delivering your work accountabilities. This is you with all the stops out.

Buffer days are looser. You may be winding down from one project and preparing for the next, doing some reflection or research, maybe some routine housekeeping, catching up with people in your network, and allowing yourself an early exit for some rest and recuperation.

Then there are Free days. Free days are when for 24 hours work ceases utterly to exist. You zap even the stealthiest little work thought. Your laptop is not just closed, but switched off, packed away in its case and shoved under the bed out of sight. You throw your work phone and BlackBerry to the bottom of a very deep, soundproof well.

And you are free. Free to be a partner, a parent, a gardener, a potter-abouter, a tennis player, a chess-master, a hiker, an art enthusiast, a TV-addict, a sports fan, a lazy slob – all the things you are when you are not working.

Warning: if you allow even one work thought to creep over your inner garden wall, if you sneak into your bedroom for even the tiniest peek at your emails, if you take even the briefest and most mundane calls about work – bang! – it's not a Free day anymore. It's a Buffer day.

When I heard this I realised something awful: I'd not had a single Free day since I started working at 16!

And I know I'm not alone.

But by making hard choices and developing good time habits I started to increase the number of Free days I had. It wasn't easy but I kept at it.

Hard choices about what? Accountabilities. What are your core accountabilities, to yourself, your family, and your employer? Think carefully about this. For your core accountabilities at work, chances are the job description in your contract is already out of date. What is the final, end-of-the-day measure of success as it relates to your core work accountabilities?

Sometimes it takes scarily frank chats with your boss to define them. And remember, your boss is probably just as rubbish at time as you are, and her vision may be just as clouded. So, probably, are the people you're supposed to be managing, the ones whose job it is to help you achieve your core accountabilities.

Persevere. Once you've nailed your core work accountabilities, imagine having *enough time* to fulfil them properly, being able to bring all your talents and experience to bear, all your skill and judgement. What a great job you could do! Imagine having the *leisure* to *do your job well!*

Okay. Now imagine you could only work five hours a day. That's all. By some freakish outturn of events it is now *against the law* to work more than five hours a day. Work more than that and you and your family will be bunged in prison. And yet, your core accountabilities haven't changed! You're given no leeway whatsoever. You must deliver exactly the same result and you've only got five hours a day in which to do it!

Start shedding. Shedding what? Go big here. Don't write to-do lists. That's tinkering around the edges. Go to the source of time-banditry. Shed *commitments*, not *tasks*. Any commitment that does not feed into a core accountability – out the door! Be prepared for consternation and upset. Most people are focused on process, not outcomes, because process is way easier.

(I've just had a horrible thought. What if most people don't actually know what their core accountabilities are? Or worse, they know, all too well, but aren't up to it? Paul often says many executives have *too much* time on their hands, which is why they sit in pointless meetings, push non-essential emails around and generally tie themselves up in process. We once coached a guy who complained bitterly about the hours he worked and yet he'd think nothing of driving 90 minutes down the M25 and 90 minutes back for a 20-minute meeting. How much of our busy-ness is just hiding from the fact we don't know what we're supposed to be doing?)

I've done the core accountability exercise and it's absolutely fascinating – and liberating. The mist clears. The *stuff* you need to *do* – the information you need to find, the reports you need to write, the problems you need to work on, the people you need to connect with – all stand out like Himalayan peaks glittering in the sunshine.

Now, habits. Good time habits. Notice I don't say "discipline". That's because successful people have successful habits, and unsuccessful people have unsuccessful habits. Whatever habits we have, we are 100% disciplined to them.

Here are three good time habits:

1. Wean yourself off the teat of electronic communications. As a starting point, switch off your phone and BlackBerry and quit Outlook or whatever email programme you run for two hours every morning and two hours every afternoon. "A wealth of information creates a poverty of attention," wrote Herbert Simon, Nobel Prize-winning economist. Clear time to think. Move up the information hierarchy from data and information to knowledge and wisdom.
2. Be very, very selective about what you promise. Get used to saying 'No.' Promise only what supports your core accountabilities, and only what you can deliver.
3. Treat time as the precious resource it is, for you and others. Be on time and keep to schedules. Meetings usually go over time because somebody's taking their ego out

for a spin. Is it you?

"Most of you guys act like you're going to live forever," a wise man said to Paul nearly 20 years ago.

I often forget and start squandering time, but I'm doing a lot better now than when I first heard about Free days. Now I have around 30 Free days every quarter. And my business is three times bigger than it was when I had no Free days.

Here are some questions to get you started looking at your own habits.

1. Do you behave as if time is *the* most precious resource you have?
2. What habits, if you dropped them, would give you more time?
3. What habits, if you adopted them, would give you more time for the important stuff?
4. If you had one year left, what changes would you make right now, no delay?

BE A TIME LORD

 Power tool n° 19

1. Each hour, on the hour, make a note of what you're doing.
2. At the end of the day look at your eight or 10 jottings and ask, for each one: is that the best use of my time, given my position, salary, purpose and goals?
3. Adjust accordingly.
4. Repeat once a week until it becomes a habit.

20. The Transparent Leader

WHO NEEDS THAT SORT OF BUM-BITING KARMA?

The root cause of struggle and wasted energy is usually somebody not telling their truth.

Okay, let's be honest - construction is a really hard business to be transparent in. In a world where the contract is everything, and where it's negotiated to within a micron of the humanly possible, you can hardly make a cup of tea without disturbing some 'commercial sensitivity' or other.

I know...

I *know*!

But still, it's better to be straight. Here's why.

It's better for you.

Lying eats up vast amounts of energy. For one thing, it takes up a lot more brain power. When you lie you create an alternative world and to keep this fake world turning you have to keep filling it with lies. You have to stay two or three steps ahead of everybody you lie to. We've probably all had a taste of that, even if only as children, and we know how exhausting it is. Lying is also terribly draining, emotionally. We long to connect with people, and if we're feeding them lies we pretend to connect without really connecting. That, also, is exhausting.

We were doing a workshop once with the board of a company and the subject came up, all on its own. When is it acceptable to tell a lie, I asked? The conversation took off. People usually have something to say about that. After a few minutes one executive boasted that he lied all the time to clients. He was so good at it they could never tell he was lying.

I was a little taken aback. Okay, I said, you're good at lying, but at what cost, to yourself? He went quiet for the rest of that session. After the next session he came up to me and said I'd opened a whole can of worms. He said he'd been in the industry 35 years and had five to go and wasn't sure at all whether he wanted to go on. He also said he hadn't had a decent night's sleep in years.

It's better for business relationships.

The calculation we make when telling a lie is, can I get away with it for long *enough*? Long enough for the transaction to close and for it to be too late for come-back? Long enough for other considerations to come in and take precedence over the lie? Long enough for people to forget, or for the ones who remember to somehow go away? The answer is, you can never tell.

I have personal - painful - experience of this. I was helping bid for a major project and the clincher was whether we'd put this particular bloke on the job. The client liked and trusted him. We weren't going to because he was needed elsewhere. (After all, liked and trusted people are rare and valuable.)

But we said we would.

At the first few meetings the client grilled me relentlessly: where's our bloke? We made excuses. The job got underway, and I moved on to other things in the company. But a year later I got on a train and spotted the client. We saw each other and there was an empty seat beside him so I went and sat down. He seemed ill at ease. After some stilted small talk I asked him where he was going.

"Dave," he said, "I have to say I was hoping you wouldn't sit here, but I might as well tell you. I'm going to one of the regular industry meetings we have where the MDs get together and discuss issues we've been having. We never trusted you guys after you spun us a line. That's the sort of thing we're going to be talking about, and I honestly can't imagine your company getting work in this sector again."

Fortunately it was a short train ride!

He may have been exaggerating, or maybe not, but either way who needs that sort of bum-biting karma?

I have a happier story. On one job word got out from the accounts department that a particular subcontractor wasn't going to be paid, though he was due a lot - £1.5 million. You're supposed to toe the party line and keep shtum, but this really didn't sit right with me.

I was faced with a dilemma: tell them and watch them walk off site at a critical time, or say nothing and wait for the fall-out when they saw the money wasn't in the bank. Without much further thought I did the unthinkable. I rang up their director, took a deep breath, and told him I was going to spoil his day. Then I blurted out that it was going to be at least two weeks before he saw any of that money, which I knew he needed as badly as we did.

After a pause he said: "You haven't ruined my day. You've made my week. Nobody ever tells me this. I have to go around calling and chasing to find out what's happening, and usually I can't. Now I can plan for it."

That was 15 years ago, and I still have a great relationship with that director. In fact, he's one of our customers now. Being straight develops trust, and who knows where trust will take a relationship?

It makes you a better leader.

Having a 'what you see is what you get' style makes it easier to enrol people in a tricky venture. If you're transparent, people don't spend time guessing what your agenda is. If you're comfortable lying to other people it only follows that you're going to lie to them, doesn't it? So either they know what's going on and are hacked off with you for not coming clean or they're making up their own stories and spreading gossip - the cancer that eats through a business.

Remember the guy who boasted about his skill at lying? It turned out nobody in his team trusted him. They could hear him all day on the phone, lying. One of his people told me: "If he's lying to them he's probably lying to me, too."

Being transparent is not the same as letting it all hang out, like in the film "Meet the Fockers", when the hapless Greg has his drink spiked with 'truth serum' the day before his wedding. In a project or venture certain truths matter and certain truths don't. What takes skill, and wisdom, and seriousness, is telling the difference. A colleague's dress sense maybe doesn't. A colleague's propensity to get drunk at clients' functions maybe does.

It also takes fortitude. Often you can tell the issue that needs a shot of transparency by the number of wasps buzzing around it.

About 10 years ago, in the early days of partnering, I got a call from a contractor who was at loggerheads with the client's team, to the point where he'd submitted a fatuous claim just to get them to sit up and listen - which of course hadn't worked.

My response was to get the key players in a room to talk about it. So we got the key players together - the client, the client's team (designers and various consultants), the contractor and half-a-dozen of the most important subcontractors. There were about 25 people in the room. The job was supposed to be a partnership, and it was week 28 of a 60-week project. The contractor had started the job, and was working proactively, but for various reasons the client had started to change the project. The contractor was taking on board the changes and in his monthly valuations submitting his variation account. Naturally he wanted to be paid for the variations. But the cost consultant kept rejecting the variation account, crossing whole chunks out without explanation.

In the workshop we split people into their groups, putting the client, design team, contractor and subcontractors in four separate corners. I asked, if you could start again what would you do differently? I floated around listening and they were all saying the same thing: they wished they could get these issues on the table and sort them out, but felt they couldn't because it might spoil the partnership. So they were all withholding, and some of them were being deliberately obscure.

I got them back into one group, told them what I'd heard, and asked how they thought the health of this partnership was. Most gave an uncomfortable laugh, seeing it was already spoilt by not having straight conversations.

Exploring further, the view in the room was that 'partnership' was about being *nice* to each other. Straight talking and difficult conversations was not being *nice*. (I can vouch that it's still the view now.) So I said, "Look, you're in week 28 of 60, so you can have your time again. Are you up for having some difficult conversations right now?" The resounding answer was yes. So, for about three hours they had some really difficult conversations and, as often happens in the right environment, they sorted it out. The second half of the project was very different and turned out to be a great success.

We see the words "open and honest" engraved in loads of so-called 'partnership charters', which get solemnly drafted at the start of a project, framed, hung on the wall, and forgotten. We chose the word 'transparent' over 'honest' because the opposite of transparent is opaque, and you can be honest, technically, even as you're obscuring important parts of the whole picture. The default setting out there seems to be "Well, as long as I'm not telling an actual lie and what I'm saying is accurate then that's all right."

As coaches we find that where vast amounts of energy are wasted in struggle it's usually because transparency is lacking. Where there is a culture of concealment what gets blocked is not information - information always gets out - but trust, and trust is the vital lubricant of any project or venture.

This is something you can fix. People rarely lie because they're liars by nature. The funny thing about the truth is that it's actually very serviceable - people usually lie or obfuscate because they haven't found what feels like the right way to say their truth. We work with people behind the scenes and help them find the right words and spirit to be clear and transparent. The most common response they get is, "How come it took you so long?"

THE WINDSCREEN WIPER

 Power tool n° 20

1. Make a note of a work situation that is bogged down, difficult and draining your energy.
2. Next to it identify the way or the ways in which you are being less than transparent.
3. Script out the things you can say to the person or people involved that will create transparency.
4. Create the opportunity and work it deliberately into the conversation.
5. Repeat as necessary.

21. The Unreasonable Leader

THOSE LIMITS YOU SMACK UP AGAINST: ARE THEY REALLY YOUR LIMITS?

"The reasonable man adapts himself to the world: the unreasonable one persists in trying to adapt the world to himself. Therefore all progress depends on the unreasonable man."
- George Bernard Shaw

The most serious crime in the workshops of Thomas Edison was going to sleep, according to his biographers. Edison himself worked 18 hours a day, pulling the occasional three-day stretch, and he expected no less from his staff. If he caught you napping he'd employ the 'resurrecter of the dead', a small explosive device that set you on fire. In a more benevolent mood he'd use the 'corpse reviver', an ear-splitting noise-maker let off by your head.

We think of Edison as an inventor but really he ran one of the world's most successful patent factories which, at its peak, employed over 200 machinists, scientists and craftsmen, organised into groups all working on the next big thing. Thanks to Edison we got the phonograph, the electric light bulb, electricity distribution and improved telephone and motion picture technology. He was like a one-man technological revolution, except it wasn't just one man – he had all these people working for him who were equally as driven.

Today his management style would get him arrested for assault or at least sued for constructive dismissal, and fair enough. But he does illustrate an important point, which is that unless you're prepared to smoke people out of their comfort zones you'll never harness their true potential, and big results will pass you by.

Smoking people out of their comfort zones – and you too, out of your own comfort zone – is the splendid art of unreasonableness.

When we started crystallising our thoughts on this Paul and I resorted to examples drawn from hard physical activity, Paul from his experience with the Royal Marines PTI programme and both of us from our marathon and triathlon habits. Stuff like 'muscle tissue doesn't grow stronger unless it's torn by hard training' and other kinds of gung-ho slogans bubbled naturally to the surface.

But we found this didn't really nail what we meant. In fact, one of the problems this industry has is precisely its tendency to solve issues by doing things *harder* and *faster*. The last thing we need is more hours, more stress and more struggle.

In fact, the comfort zones we need to disrupt are usually not even that *comfortable*. I once had a project manager who was a fantastic bloke and really hard worker, but he couldn't delegate. Because he was good, he'd been given loads of responsibility – a difficult inner-city job, plus mopping up other old jobs, and also the company's own HQ refurb, which is a poisoned chalice at the best of times. On top of all that his wife had recently given birth to twins.

One day he burst into my office and said, 'My life's in tatters! I can't do everything. I need to know what's priority.' Being a nice person I nearly stopped everything to go through with him what could be offloaded. But something made me stop. "No," I said. "I want you to do it all. That's what I'm paying you for. I want you to go away and think about it and tell me what support you need."

I could see his eyes welling up in the instant before he stormed out of the room, slamming the door behind him. I felt terrible. But two hours later he came back, calmer, and said, 'Right, I know where you're coming from....' and listed the support he needed – including for me to roll my sleeves up and get involved. He'd finally got it into his head that he couldn't do everything himself. He admitted later he thought I was being totally unreasonable and that he'd never had a boss refuse to prioritise his own commitments for him.

What this shows is that sometimes the comfort zone you need to disrupt isn't laziness, but a thought habit that is self-defeating or counter-productive. Or those less-than-honest little self-justifications we use, privately, to let ourselves off the hook. "But look at the hours I work!", "If *somebody* would just tell me what's going on…!", "I *said* this would happen two months ago…", "That's not *really* in my job description…", and so on.

One way of pushing yourself and your team to higher levels is to implement a technique called Request-and-Promise. It's simple enough, on the face of it. You make a request, and your colleague has four choices. She or he can say:

1. **Yes.** This means, yup, you'll do it. It's pull out all the stops time. And you'd better do it or your credibility goes downhill fast.
2. **Yes, if…** This means yes, but you need a promise in return, such as an essential bit of information, an introduction, cover for something, whatever.
3. **Yes, but…** This means yes, but with modifications, such as not by the time you want or not exactly in the way you want.
4. **No.** This is a beautiful trump card which must be respected. The only caveat is, the more you use it in a Request-and-Promise environment the more people will start to wonder what you're doing there.

Oh, and one more thing: the 'request' in a Request-and-Promise leadership environment is a 'stretching' request, not just another task for your to-do list.

I've seen this take root for a time in two different national contractors and it was very unreasonable – and absolutely *rockin*! The normal hierarchies went out the window. My boss was 'managing' me by request and promise and I was doing the same to him, and it was happening off to either side of us, and up and down in the seniority chain, and even out to some of our key subcontractors. Often the requests were just too much, and you'd have to rely, and I mean really rely, on the team around you. And because everyone was in the same boat there was a lot of bending over backwards going on. The result was fantastic team work and extraordinary results.

Here's an example. I was in charge of rolling out a national change programme and my boss called me up and asked how it was going. I gave a vague, anecdotal sort of response. He said no, he needed hard data – hard, comprehensive data.

"Can you get me that by the end of the month?" he asked.

(Request.)

"Yup," I said.

(Promise.)

Then I put the phone down and wondered how on earth I was going to do an audit worth the paper it was written on, of over a hundred construction sites all over the country, in – I looked at the calendar – less than three weeks. It was impossible! I did the only thing I could think of and sent an email out to all construction and contract managers saying, more or less, "Help!". I didn't know what I was hoping for. These were senior people with tons on their plates and no obvious reason to drop everything and help me. In fact, many would have been justified in viewing me and my prying questions with suspicion.

But an astounding thing happened. Within a few days I had 20 of them in a room, willing at least to hear me out. A little nervously, I explained the background to the programme and what I'd been asked to do. They conferred for a while. Then one said: "Dave, do you think you could take yourself off somewhere for a couple of hours?" "Sure," I said. I found a spare desk, made some calls, sent some emails and puzzled over what they were up to. Those two hours took a long time. When they were finally up I went back and found them chatting easily and getting caught up.

"How's it going?" I said.

"Oh, hi Dave," they said, and handed me a file. "There's your audit."

As a team culture, Request-and-Promise is far more effective than its opposite, one based on instructions. With the latter you're a policeman and all your energy goes into hounding, monitoring and punishing. A Request-and-Promise culture takes skill to set up and foster. For instance, there's a fine line between delegating by request and indiscriminate dumping. Everybody has to know what's going on and there needs to be an atmosphere of trust and cooperation. But done right, Request-and-Promise is like rocket fuel in a board, team or organisation.

Note: Being unreasonable is not the same as being disagreeable. You can be unreasonable and still show courtesy, respect and consideration. Being disagreeable merely tells the world that your personal evolution is low on your priority list.

Being unreasonable with yourself can mean:

- Sticking to your principles when the reasonable thing to do would be to cave in. (Groucho Marx said: "These are my principles and if you don't like them... well, I have others.")
- Not believing your own twaddle about being too old, too young, not smart enough, not qualified enough
- Taking responsibility for everything you do *and* for your response to what is *done to you*
- Realising that the time for learning and growing will never be over
- Answering back to the voice in your head that says it's okay to renege, to cut corners, to mislead, etc.
- Being unreasonable with others can mean:
- Having the bottle to let them struggle to reach their own solutions. You can't

do someone's gym session for them, nor can you teach them the meaning of disappointment
- Intolerance toward indifference or bad habits – being late for meetings, being sloppy with presentations, being lazy about learning something small but important
- Shining a light on behaviour or attitudes that are holding them back
- Impatience with 'More of the Same'

GO AGAINST THE FLOW

1. Do the Self and Others exercise above. Honestly rate your unreasonableness.
2. Make yourself a Mr. Unreasonable script. Write down: "You and I both know that's not good enough." Underneath, write the same thing 10 different ways (without being disagreeable). Memorise these statements and practice them out loud. Get the words and you'll get the confidence. Plus, being able to say the same thing in different ways gets people's attention without you sounding crazy.
3. Do an audit of your own leadership style. Assign a ratio to the amount of Requests you make versus Instructions. If it's weighted towards Instructions, introduce more Requests, and watch the energy, commitment and results in your team rise.

Further reading: The toughest limits are always in our heads and hearts, in the realms of thought and emotion. If you want smarter work - as opposed to harder work - from yourself and your team, this is the area to target. A good place to start (among many) is *Leadership and Self-deception: Getting Out of the Box*, by The Arbinger Institute.

Afterword
IT'S DOWN TO US

By Dave Stitt

The management ethos Baby Boomers like me inherited, and perpetuated, was based on a command-and-control ("bark, bollock and bite") model, where decisions were made at the top and enforced down the line, where hierarchies were protected and the culture was combative and macho. We still expect young men (they're pretty much all still men) to work day and night and sacrifice any sort of life outside their jobs. We get people to do things by sticks and carrots – verbal abuse and banishment from the club for failure, and money and perks for success.

I know this intimately because that's what I was like. Throughout the 80s and early 90s I was a fast-rising project manager. I didn't necessarily like the prevailing culture but that's the way it was and I was ambitious and versatile so I absorbed it. One of the reasons I was so keen to rise up the management ladder was to stop being on the receiving end so much! And by the standards of the time I was okay as a manager. I was award-winning, in fact, even though I realise now how much time, energy and money got wasted in my struggle and conflict.

But even back then there were visionary people trying to change things. I was lucky enough to be asked to help roll out a culture change programme with a national contractor, bringing in approaches from outside to try shift the focus from short-term results to long-term relationships and in so doing to cut out some of this built-in dysfunction. I found it tremendously exciting. My eyes were opened to a whole new world! I went on to lead a similar programme for another national contractor before setting up my performance coaching business in 2001.

The fruits of those change programmes are still rolling on today, 10 years on. At the heart of them are enlightened individuals – leaders – who know how to foster engagement, commitment and true talent in their teams.

There's been more than enough discussion in the last 20 years about what's "wrong" with construction. We have had some good reports with sensible recommendations as well as a fair amount of blame. It's the fault of the clients, or the designers, or the QSs or the contractors. All sorts of procurement systems and forms of contract have been proposed to "fix" the industry, though the silver bullet cure remains elusive.

The reality is, if you work in or lead a construction business today you can't just wait for some sort of systemic change to come along and alter conditions more to your favour. You have to lead the change.

When I was a thrusting young project manager I was always pestering my boss for the next promotion, to contracts manager. I wanted the title and the car and the prestige that went with it. Then one day I realised that if I wanted to have all the trappings of a contracts manager, I'd better start acting like one - being more responsible, more diplomatic, more thoughtful, more strategic. And then, as if by magic, I became one.

I carried that lesson with me and it informs every part of this book. To borrow from Ghandi, be the change you want to see.

About the authors

Dave Stitt BSc (Hons) CEng MICE FCIOB MCMI FRSA

Dave left school at 16 and stumbled into a job as a chain boy. He then joined Taylor Woodrow as a trainee engineer and with hard work and a world class training programme he rose through the ranks to project manager. After 15 years with Taylor Woodrow he joined Birse and gained promotion to the northern regional business board responsible for operations. Involvement in the Birse Transformation Programme shifted his career from operations to people, performance and change. He then joined Wates and led their award winning Improving Construction Programme which enhanced culture and profit.

Inspired to change the construction industry, Dave established DSA Building Performance Ltd in 2001 which coaches individuals, teams and organisations to identify and achieve big results.

Paul Fox MSc

Over the past 15 years Paul has pioneered coaching as a business tool in the construction sector, and has a proven track record of helping people and organisations raise their productivity and performance. Paul works at the highest level, coaching managing directors, COOs and business owners. Clients have included Aedas, Atkins, Balfour Beatty, Carillion, The Highways Agency, Mace and PBA.

Paul has spent thousands of hours both in board and workshop settings and hundreds of hours in one-to-one coaching conversations. He has led internal change programmes for a major contractor and helped design and deliver leadership initiatives in some of the organisations above.

Before becoming a full-time coach, Paul was Group People Development Manager for Birse. His unique insights on enhancing performance come from a multi-sector career – he has been an engineer, a civil servant and a Royal Marine.

DSA Building Performance

The DSA team of experienced associates helps individuals, teams and organisations achieve more. DSA's suite of services include:

- Board-level leadership team improvement
- Merger, acquisition and joint venture integration
- Project team improvement
- Essential practice implementation

For more information visit www.dsabuilding.co.uk